Your Office

Advanced Problem Solving Cases

Amy Kinser

J. ERIC KINSER

JENNIFER NIGHTINGALE MASSART

Boston Columbus Indianapolis New York San Francisco Amsterdam Cape Town
Dubai London Madrid Milan Munich Paris Montréal Toronto Delhi Mexico City
São Paulo Sydney Hong Kong Seoul Singapore Taipei Tokyo

Editorial Director: Andrew Gilfillan
Senior Portfolio Manager: Samantha McAfee Lewis
Team Lead, Project Management: Laura Burgess
Project Manager: Anne Garcia
Development Editor: N. Lamm Consulting Associates, Ltd.
Portfolio Management Assistant: Michael Campbell
Director of Product Marketing: Maggie Waples
Director of Field Marketing: Leigh Ann Sims
Product Marketing Manager: Kaylee Carlson
Field Marketing Managers: Joanna Conley & Molly Schmidt
Marketing Assistant: Kelli Fisher
Senior Operations Specialist: Maura Zaldivar-Garcia

Senior Art Director: Mary Siener
Manager, Permissions: Gina Cheselka
Interior and Cover Design: Studio Montage
Cover Photo: Rawpixel.com/Shutterstock
Associate Director of Design: Blair Brown
MyLab Product Model Manager: Eric Hakanson
Vice President, Product Management, MyLab: Jason Fournier
Digital Product Manager: Heather Darby
Media Project Manager, Production: John Cassar
Full-Service Project Management: Cenveo Publisher Services
Composition: Cenveo Publisher Services
Chapter opener image: Flowerstock/Shutterstock

Credits and acknowledgments borrowed from other sources and reproduced, with permission, in this textbook appear on appropriate page within text.

Pearson Education Ltd., London
Pearson Education Singapore, Pte. Ltd
Pearson Education, Canada, Inc.
Pearson Education–Japan

Pearson Education Australia PTY, Limited
Pearson Education North Asia Ltd., Hong Kong
Pearson Educación de Mexico, S.A. de C.V.
Pearson Education Malaysia, Pte. Ltd.

Library of Congress Cataloging-in-Publication Data available upon request

1 16
ISBN-10: 0-13-448095-3
ISBN-13: 978-0-13-448095-4

Dedications

I dedicate this series to my Kinser Boyz for their unwavering love, support, and patience; to my parents and sister for their love; to my students for inspiring me; to Sam for believing in me; and to the instructors I hope this series will inspire!

Amy S. Kinser

For my wife, Amy, and our two boys, Matt and Aidan. I cannot thank them enough for their support, love, and endless inspiration.

J. Eric Kinser

To my parents, who always believed in and encouraged me. To my husband and best friend, who gave me support, patience, and love. To my brother and my hero—may you be watching from Heaven with joy in your heart.

Jennifer Nightingale Massart

About the Authors

Amy S. Kinser, Esq., Series Editor

Amy holds a B.A. degree in Chemistry with a Business minor from Indiana University, and a J.D. from the Maurer School of Law, also at Indiana University. After working as an environmental chemist, starting her own technology consulting company, and practicing intellectual property law, she has spent the past 15 years teaching technology at the Kelley School of Business in Bloomington, Indiana. Currently, she serves as the Director of Computer Skills and Senior Lecturer at the Kelley School of Business at Indiana University. She also loves spending time with her two sons, Aidan and J. Matthew, and her husband J. Eric.

J. Eric Kinser

Eric Kinser received his B.S. degree in Biology from Indiana University and his M.S. in Counseling and Education from the Indiana School of Education. He has worked in the medical field and in higher education as a technology and decision support specialist. He is currently a senior lecturer in the Operations and Decision Technology Department at the Kelley School of Business at Indiana University. When not teaching he enjoys experimenting with new technologies, traveling, and hiking with his family.

Jennifer Nightingale Massart

Jennifer Nightingale Massart, associate professor at Slippery Rock University, has taught Information Systems Management since 2000. Before entering academia, she spent 15 years in industry with a focus in management and training. Her research expertise is in instructional technology, using technology as a teaching tool, and the impact of instructional technologies on student learning. She has earned numerous teaching and research honors and awards, holds an Ed.D. (instructional technology) and two M.S. degrees (information systems management and education) from Duquesne University, and has a B.A. from the University of Pittsburgh. She lives in the suburbs north of Pittsburgh with her husband, Chuck, and cat, Allie.

Contents

Business concepts are explored and applied throughout the cases in this book as follows:

Business Concept	Case
Business Analytics	Integrated Access & Excel 3
Business Models	Access 1
Business Process Mapping	Access 5
Components of a Spreadsheet Model (Inputs, Outputs, Decision Variables, and Uncertain Variables)	Excel 1
Cost of Lost Profits	Excel 3
Dashboards	Excel 6
Data Types (Discrete, Continuous, Nominal, Ordinal, and Interval)	Integrated Access & Excel 3
Decision Support Systems	Excel 2
Depreciating Assets	Excel 5
Economic Order Quantity (EOQ)	Excel 4
Evaluating Software Systems (CRM, SCM, ERP, and Custom)	Integrated Access & Excel 2
Feasibility Analysis	Integrated Access & Excel 2
Heuristics	Excel 3
Horizontal Versus Vertical Market	Integrated Access & Excel 2
Implementation Strategies	Access 2 & 6
Key Performance Indicators (KPIs)	Integrated Access & Excel 3
Linking Applications	Integrated Access & Excel 1
Loan Analysis	Excel 5
Management Pyramid (Strategic, Tactical, and Operational)	Excel 2
Nature of Data and Data Cleansing	Integrated Access & Excel 1
Normalization	Access 6
Phases of Decision Making (Intelligence, Design, and Choice)	Excel 2
Porter's Five Forces	Excel 6
Porter's Four Competitive Strategies	Excel 6
Probability Distributions and Business Statistics	Excel 5
Professional Reporting	Access 4
Providing Business Information with Advanced Queries	Access 3
Regression	Integrated Access & Excel 3
Scenario Manager	Excel 4
Sensitivity and Risk Analysis	Excel 3
Simulation and Predictive Modeling	Excel 3; also Integrated Access & Excel 3
Solver	Excel 4
Spreadsheet Design (Accuracy, Clarity, Flexibility, Efficiency, and Documentation)	Excel 1
Statistical Relationships (Linear, Nonlinear, Positive, Negative, and None)	Integrated Access & Excel 3
Systems Development Life Cycle (SDLC) and Business Requirements	Access 2
Usability and Useful Forms	Access 4 & 6
Web Metrics and Pricing	Integrated Access & Excel 3

Acknowledgments

The **Your Office** team would like to thank the following reviewers who have invested time and energy to help shape this series from the very beginning, providing us with invaluable feedback through their comments, suggestions, and constructive criticism.

We'd like to thank all of our conscientious reviewers, including those who contributed to our previous editions:

Sven Aelterman
Troy University

Nitin Aggarwal
San Jose State University

Heather Albinger
Waukesha County Technical College

Angel Alexander
Piedmont Technical College

Melody Alexander
Ball State University

Karen Allen
Community College of Rhode Island

Maureen Allen
Elon University

Wilma Andrews
Virginia Commonwealth University

Mazhar Anik
Owens Community College

David Antol
Harford Community College

Kirk Atkinson
Western Kentucky University

Barbara Baker
Indiana Wesleyan University

Kristi Berg
Minot State University

Kavuri Bharath
Old Dominion University

Ann Blackman
Parkland College

Jeanann Boyce
Montgomery College

Lynn Brooks
Tyler Junior College

Cheryl Brown
Delgado Community College West Bank Campus

Bonnie Buchanan
Central Ohio Technical College

Peggy Burrus
Red Rocks Community College

Richard Cacace
Pensacola State College

Margo Chaney
Carroll Community College

Shanan Chappell
College of the Albemarle, North Carolina

Kuan-Chou Chen
Purdue University, Calumet

David Childress
Ashland Community and Technical College

Keh-Wen Chuang
Purdue University North Central

Suzanne Clayton
Drake University

Amy Clubb
Portland Community College

Bruce Collins
Davenport University

Linda Collins
Mesa Community College

Margaret Cooksey
Tallahassee Community College

Charmayne Cullom
University of Northern Colorado

Christy Culver
Marion Technical College

Juliana Cypert
Tarrant County College

Harold Davis
Southeastern Louisiana University

Jeff Davis
Jamestown Community College

Jennifer Day
Sinclair Community College

Anna Degtyareva
Mt. San Antonio College

Beth Deinert
Southeast Community College

Kathleen DeNisco
Erie Community College

Donald Dershem
Mountain View College

Sallie Dodson
Radford University

Joseph F. Domagala
Duquesne University

Bambi Edwards
Craven Community College

Elaine Emanuel
Mt. San Antonio College

Diane Endres
Ancilla College

Nancy Evans
Indiana University, Purdue University, Indianapolis

Christa Fairman
Arizona Western College

Marni Ferner
University of North Carolina, Wilmington

Paula Fisher
Central New Mexico Community College

Linda Fried
University of Colorado, Denver

Diana Friedman
Riverside Community College

Susan Fry
Boise State University

Virginia Fullwood
Texas A&M University, Commerce

Janos Fustos
Metropolitan State College of Denver

John Fyfe
University of Illinois at Chicago

Saiid Ganjalizadeh
The Catholic University of America

Randolph Garvin
Tyler Junior College

Diane Glowacki
Tarrant County College

Jerome Gonnella
Northern Kentucky University

Lorie Goodgine
Tennessee Technology Center in Paris

Connie Grimes
Morehead State University

Debbie Gross
Ohio State University

Babita Gupta
California State University, Monterey Bay

Lewis Hall
Riverside City College

Jane Hammer
Valley City State University

Marie Hartlein
Montgomery County Community College

Darren Hayes
Pace University

Paul Hayes
Eastern New Mexico University

Mary Hedberg
Johnson County Community College

Lynda Henrie
LDS Business College

Deedee Herrera
Dodge City Community College

Marilyn Hibbert
Salt Lake Community College

Jan Hime
University of Nebraska, Lincoln

Cheryl Hinds
Norfolk State University

Mary Kay Hinkson
Fox Valley Technical College

Margaret Hohly
Cerritos College

Brian Holbert
Spring Hill College

Susan Holland
Southeast Community College

Anita Hollander
University of Tennessee, Knoxville

Emily Holliday
Campbell University

Stacy Hollins
St. Louis Community College Florissant Valley

Mike Horn
State University of New York, Geneseo

Christie Hovey
Lincoln Land Community College

Margaret Hvatum
St. Louis Community College Meramec

Jean Insinga
Middlesex Community College

Kristyn Jacobson
Madison College

Jon (Sean) Jasperson
Texas A&M University

Glen Jenewein
Kaplan University

Gina Jerry
Santa Monica College

Dana Johnson
North Dakota State University

Mary Johnson
Mt. San Antonio College

Linda Johnsonius
Murray State University

Carla Jones
Middle Tennessee State University

Susan Jones
Utah State University

Nenad Jukic
Loyola University, Chicago

Sali Kaceli
Philadelphia Biblical University

Sue Kanda
Baker College of Auburn Hills

Robert Kansa
Macomb Community College

Susumu Kasai
Salt Lake Community College

Linda Kavanaugh
Robert Morris University

Debby Keen
University of Kentucky

Mike Kelly
Community College of Rhode Island

Melody Kiang
California State University, Long Beach

Lori Kielty
College of Central Florida

Richard Kirk
Pensacola State College

Dawn Konicek
Blackhawk Tech

John Kucharczuk
Centennial College

David Largent
Ball State University

Frank Lee
Fairmont State University

Luis Leon
University of Tennessee, Chattanooga

Freda Leonard
Delgado Community College

Julie Lewis
Baker College, Allen Park

Suhong Li
Bryant Unversity

Renee Lightner
Florida State College

John Lombardi
South University

Rhonda Lucas
Spring Hill College

Adriana Lumpkin
Midland College

Lynne Lyon
Durham College

Nicole Lytle
California State University, San Bernardino

Donna Madsen
Kirkwood Community College

Susan Maggio
Community College of Baltimore County

Michelle Mallon
Ohio State University

Kim Manning
Tallahassee Community College

Paul Martin
Harrisburg Area Community College

Cheryl Martucci
Diablo Valley College

Sebena Masline
Florida State College of Jacksonville

Sherry Massoni
Harford Community College

Lee McClain
Western Washington University

Sandra McCormack
Monroe Community College

Sue McCrory
Missouri State University

Barbara Miller
University of Notre Dame

Johnette Moody
Arkansas Tech University

Michael O. Moorman
Saint Leo University

Kathleen Morris
University of Alabama

Alysse Morton
Westminster College

Elobaid Muna
University of Maryland Eastern Shore

Jackie Myers
Sinclair Community College

Russell Myers
El Paso Community College

Bernie Negrete
Cerritos College

Melissa Nemeth
Indiana University, Purdue University, Indianapolis

Jennifer Nightingale
Duquesne University

Kathie O'Brien
North Idaho College

Michael Ogawa
University of Hawaii

Janet Olfert
North Dakota State University

Rene Pack
Arizona Western College

Patsy Parker
Southwest Oklahoma State Unversity

Laurie Patterson
University of North Carolina, Wilmington

Alicia Pearlman
Baker College

Diane Perreault
Sierra College and California State University, Sacramento

Theresa Phinney
Texas A&M University

Vickie Pickett
Midland College

Marcia Polanis
Forsyth Technical Community College

Rose Pollard
Southeast Community College

Stephen Pomeroy
Norwich University

Leonard Presby
William Paterson University

Donna Reavis
Delta Career Education

Eris Reddoch
Pensacola State College

James Reddoch
Pensacola State College

Michael Redmond
La Salle University

Terri Rentfro
John A. Logan College

Vicki Robertson
Southwest Tennessee Community College

Jennifer Robinson
Trident Technical College

Dianne Ross
University of Louisiana at Lafayette

Ann Rowlette
Liberty University

Amy Rutledge
Oakland University

Candace Ryder
Colorado State University

Joann Segovia
Winona State University

Eileen Shifflett
James Madison University

Sandeep Shiva
Old Dominion University

Robert Sindt
Johnson County Community College

Cindi Smatt
Texas A&M University

Edward Souza
Hawaii Pacific University

Nora Spencer
Fullerton College

Alicia Stonesifer
La Salle University

Jenny Lee Svelund
University of Utah

Cheryl Sypniewski
Macomb Community College

Arta Szathmary
Bucks County Community College

Nasser Tadayon
Southern Utah University

Asela Thomason
California State University Long Beach

Nicole Thompson
Carteret Community College

Terri Tiedeman
Southeast Community College, Nebraska

Lewis Todd
Belhaven University

Barb Tollinger
Sinclair Community College

Allen Truell
Ball State University

Erhan Uskup
Houston Community College

Lucia Vanderpool
Baptist College of Health Sciences

Michelle Vlaich-Lee
Greenville Technical College

Barry Walker
Monroe Community College

Rosalyn Warren
Enterprise State Community College

Sonia Washington
Prince George's Community College

Eric Weinstein
Suffolk County Community College

Jill Weiss
Florida International University

Lorna Wells
Salt Lake Community College

Rosalie Westerberg
Clover Park Technical College

Clemetee Whaley
Southwest Tennessee Community College

Kenneth Whitten
Florida State College of Jacksonville

MaryLou Wilson
Piedmont Technical College

John Windsor
University of North Texas

Kathy Winters
University of Tennessee, Chattanooga

Nancy Woolridge
Fullerton College

Jensen Zhao
Ball State University

Martha Zimmer
University of Evansville

Molly Zimmer
University of Evansville

Mary Anne Zlotow
College of DuPage

Matthew Zullo
Wake Technical Community College

Additionally, we'd like to thank our MyITLab team for their review and collaboration with our text authors:

LeeAnn Bates
MyITLab content author

Jennifer Hurley
MyITLab content author

Becca Lowe
Media Producer

Ralph Moore
MyITLab content author

Jerri Williams
MyITLab content author

Preface

Real World Problem Solving for Business and Beyond

The *Your Office* series provides the foundation for students to learn real world problem solving for use in business and beyond. Students are exposed to hands-on technical content that is woven into realistic business scenarios and focuses on using Microsoft Office as a decision-making tool.

Real world business exposure is a competitive advantage

The series features a unique running business scenario—the Painted Paradise Resort & Spa—that connects all of the cases together and exposes students to using Microsoft Office to solve problems relating to business areas such as finance and accounting, production and operations, sales and marketing, and more. Look for the icons identifying the business application of each case.

Active learning occurs in context

Each chapter introduces a realistic business case for students to complete via hands-on steps that are easily identified in blue-shaded boxes. Each blue box teaches a skill and comes complete with video, interactive, and live auto-graded support with automatic feedback.

Coursework that is relevant to students and their future careers

Real World Advice, Real World Interview Videos, and Real World Success Stories are woven throughout the text and in the student resources. These share how former students use the Microsoft Office concepts they learned in this class and had success in a variety of careers.

Outcomes matter

Whether it's getting a good grade in this course, learning how to use Excel to be successful in other courses, or learning business skills that will support success in a future job, every student has an outcome in mind. And outcomes matter. That is why we added a Business Unit opener to focus on the outcomes students will achieve by working through the cases and content of each chapter as well as the Capstone at the end of each unit.

No matter what career students may choose to pursue in life, this series will give them the foundation to succeed. And as they learn these valuable problem-solving and decision-making skills while becoming proficient in using Microsoft Office as a tool, they will achieve their intended outcomes, making a positive impact on their lives.

Key Features

The **Outcomes focus** allows students and instructors to focus on higher-level learning goals and how those can be achieved through particular objectives and skills.

- **Outcomes** are written at the course level and the business unit level.
- **Chapter Objectives list** identifies the learning objectives to be achieved as students work through the chapter. Page numbers are included for easy reference. These are revisited in the Concepts Check at the end of the chapter.
- **MOS Certification Guide** for instructors and students directs anyone interested in prepping for the MOS exam to the specific series resources to find all content required for the test.

The **real world focus** reminds students that what they are learning is practical and useful the minute they leave the classroom.

Business Application Icons

Customer Service

Finance & Accounting

General Business

Human Resources

Information Technology

Production & Operations

Sales & Marketing

Research & Development

Soft Skills

- **Real World Success** features in the chapter opener share anecdotes from real former students, describing how knowledge of Office has helped them be successful in their lives.
- **Real World Advice boxes** offer notes on best practices for general use of important Office skills. The goal is to advise students as a manager might in a future job.
- **Business Application icons** appear with every case in the text and clearly identify which business application students are being exposed to (finance, marketing, operations, etc.).

Features for active learning help students learn by doing and immerse them in the business world using Microsoft Office.

- **Blue boxes** represent the hands-on portion of the chapter and help students quickly identify what steps they need to take to complete the chapter Prepare case. This material is easily distinguishable from explanatory text by the blue-shaded background.
- **Starting and ending files** appear before every case in the text. Starting files identify exactly which student data files are needed to complete each case. Ending files are provided to show students the naming conventions they should use when saving their files. Each file icon is color coded by application.
- **Side Note** conveys a brief tip or piece of information aligned visually with a step in the chapter, quickly providing key information to students completing that particular step.
- **Consider This** offers critical thinking questions and topics for discussion, set apart as a boxed feature, allowing students to step back from the project and think about the application of what they are learning and how these concepts might be used in the future.
- **Soft Skills icons** appear with other boxed features and identify specific places where students are being exposed to lessons on soft skills.

Study aids help students review and retain the material so they can recall it at a moment's notice.

- **Quick Reference boxes** summarize generic or alternative instructions on how to accomplish a task. This feature enables students to quickly find important skills.

- **Concept Check** review questions, which appear at the end of the chapter, require students to demonstrate their understanding of the objectives.

- **Visual Summary** offers a review of the objectives learned in the chapter using images from the completed solution file, mapped to the chapter objectives with callouts and page references, so students can easily find the section of text to refer to for a refresher.

Extensive cases allow students to progress from a basic understanding of Office through to proficiency.

- **Chapters all conclude with Practice, Problem Solve, and Perform Cases** to allow full mastery at the chapter level. Alternative versions of these cases are available in Instructor Resources.

- **Business Unit Capstones all include More Practice, Problem Solve, and Perform Cases** that require students to synthesize objectives from the two previous chapters to extend their mastery of the content. Alternative versions of these cases are available in Instructor Resources.

- **More Grader Projects** are offered with this edition, including Prepare cases as well as Problem Solve cases at both the chapter and business unit capstone levels.

Resources

Instructor Resources

The Instructor's Resource Center, available at www.pearsonhighered.com/irc includes the following:

- Annotated Solution Files with Scorecards, which assist with grading the Prepare, Practice, Problem Solve, and Perform cases
- Data and solution files
- Rubrics in Microsoft Word format, which enable instructors to easily grade open-ended assignments with no definite solution
- Instructor Manuals that provide a detailed blueprint to achieve chapter learning objectives and outcomes and best use the unique structure of the business units

Student Resources

Student Data Files

Access the student data files needed to complete the cases in this textbook at www.pearsonhighered.com/youroffice.

MyITLab®

Available in MyITLab

- **Grader Projects** for Excel projects provide live-in-the-application assessment with immediate feedback and detailed reports for students.
- **eText** is available in some MyITLab courses.

MyITLab for Office 2016 is a solution designed by professors for professors that allows easy delivery of Office courses with defensible assessment and outcomes-based training. The new **Your Office 2016** system will seamlessly integrate online assessment, training, and projects with MyITLab for Microsoft Office 2016!

Dear Students,

If you want an edge over the competition, make it personal. Whether you love sports, travel, the stock market, or ballet, your passion is personal to you. Capitalizing on your passion leads to success. You live in a global marketplace, and your competition is global. The honors students in China exceed the total number of students in North America. Skills can help set you apart, but passion will make you stand above. Your Office is the tool to harness your passion's true potential.

In prior generations, personalization in a professional setting was discouraged. You had a "work" life and a "home" life. As the Series Editor, I write to you about the vision for *Your Office* from my laptop, on my couch, in the middle of the night when inspiration struck me. My classroom and living room are my office. Life has changed from generations before us.

So, let's get personal. My degrees are not in technology, but chemistry and law. I helped put myself through school by working full time in various jobs, including a successful technology consulting business that continues today. My generation did not grow up with computers, but I did. My father was a network administrator for the military. So, I was learning to program in Basic before anyone had played Nintendo's Duck Hunt or Tetris. Technology has always been one of my passions from a young age.

In fact, I now tell my husband: don't buy me jewelry for my birthday, buy me the latest gadget on the market!

In my first law position, I was known as the Office guru to the extent that no one gave me a law assignment for the first two months. Once I submitted the assignment, my supervisor remarked, "Wow, you don't just know how to leverage technology, but you really know the law too." I can tell you novel-sized stories from countless prior students in countless industries who gained an edge from using Office as a tool. Bringing technology to your passion makes you well rounded and a cut above the rest, no matter the industry or position.

I am most passionate about teaching, in particular teaching technology. I come from many generations of teachers, including my mother who is a kindergarten teacher. For over 12 years, I have found my dream job passing on my passion for teaching, technology, law, science, music, and life in general at the Kelley School of Business at Indiana University. I have tried to pass on the key to engaging passion to my students. I have helped them see what differentiates them from all the other bright students vying for the same jobs.

Microsoft Office is a tool. All of your competition will have learned Microsoft Office to some degree or another. Some will have learned it to an advanced level. Knowing Microsoft Office is important, but it is also fundamental. Without it, you will not be considered for a position.

Today, you step into your first of many future roles bringing Microsoft Office to your dream job working for Painted Paradise Resort & Spa. You will delve into the business side of the resort and learn how to use *Your Office* to maximum benefit.

Don't let the context of a business fool you. If you don't think of yourself as a business person, you have no need to worry. Whether you realize it or not, everything is business. If you want to be a nurse, you are entering the health care industry. If you want to be a football player in the NFL, you are entering the business of sports as entertainment. In fact, if you want to be a stay-at-home parent, you are entering the business of a family household where *Your Office* still gives you an advantage. For example, you will be able to prepare a budget in Excel and analyze what you need to do to afford a trip to Disney World!

At Painted Paradise Resort & Spa, you will learn how to make Office yours through four learning levels designed to maximize your understanding. You will Prepare, Practice, and Problem Solve your tasks. Then, you will astound when you Perform your new talents. You will be challenged through Consider This questions and gain insight through Real World Advice.

There is something more. You want success in what you are passionate about in your life. It is personal for you. In this position at Painted Paradise Resort & Spa, you will gain your personal competitive advantage that will stay with you for the rest of your life—*Your Office*.

Sincerely,
Amy Kinser
Series Editor

Painted Paradise

RESORT & SPA

Painted Paradise
Red Bluff Golf Course & Pro Shop

Painted Paradise
Turquoise Oasis Spa

Painted Paradise
Painted Treasures Gift Shop

Painted Paradise
Silver Moon Lounge

Painted Paradise
Event Planning & Catering

Painted Paradise
Indigo5 Restaurant

Welcome to the Team!

Welcome to your new office at Painted Paradise Resort & Spa, where we specialize in painting perfect getaways. As the Chief Technology Officer, I am excited to have staff dedicated to the Microsoft Office integration between all the areas of the resort. Our team is passionate about our paradise, and I hope you find this to be your dream position here!

Painted Paradise is a resort and spa in New Mexico catering to business people, romantics, families, and anyone who just needs to get away. Inside our resort are many distinct areas. Many of these areas operate as businesses in their own right but must integrate with the other areas of the resort. The main areas of the resort are as follows.

- The **Hotel** is overseen by our Chief Executive Officer, William Mattingly, and is at the core of our business. The hotel offers a variety of accommodations, ranging from individual rooms to a grand villa suite. Further, the hotel offers packages including spa, golf, and special events.

  Room rates vary according to size, season, demand, and discount. The hotel has discounts for typical groups, such as AARP. The hotel also has a loyalty program where guests can earn free nights based on frequency of visits. Guests may charge anything from the resort to the room.

- **Red Bluff Golf Course** is a private world-class golf course and pro shop. The golf course has services such as golf lessons from the famous golf pro John Schilling and playing packages. Also, the golf course attracts local residents. This requires variety in pricing schemes to accommodate both local and hotel guests. The pro shop sells many retail items online.

  The golf course can also be reserved for special events and tournaments. These special events can be in conjunction with a wedding, conference, meetings, or other events covered by the event planning and catering area of the resort.

- **Turquoise Oasis Spa** is a full-service spa. Spa services include haircuts, pedi-cures, massages, facials, body wraps, waxing, and various other spa services— typical to exotic. Further, the spa offers private consultation, weight training (in the fitness center), a water bar, meditation areas, and steam rooms. Spa services are offered both in the spa and in the resort guest's room.

  Turquoise Oasis Spa uses top-of-the-line products and some house-brand products. The retail side offers products ranging from candles to age-defying home treatments. These products can also be purchased online. Many of the hotel guests who fall in love with the house-brand soaps, lotions, candles, and other items appreciate being able to buy more at any time.

  The spa offers a multitude of packages including special hotel room packages that include spa treatments. Local residents also use the spa. So, the spa guests are not limited to hotel guests. Thus, the packages also include pricing attractive to the local community.

- **Painted Treasures Gift Shop** has an array of items available for purchase, from toiletries to clothes to presents for loved ones back home including a healthy section of kids' toys for traveling business people. The gift shop sells a small sampling from the spa, golf course pro shop, and local New Mexico culture. The gift shop also has a small section of snacks and drinks. The gift shop has numerous part-time employees including students from the local college.

- The **Event Planning & Catering** area is central to attracting customers to the resort. From weddings to conferences, the resort is a popular destination. The resort has a substantial number of staff dedicated to planning, coordinating, setting up, catering, and maintaining these events. The resort has several facilities that can accommodate large groups. Packages and prices vary by size, room, and other services such as catering. Further, the Event Planning & Catering team works closely with local vendors for floral decorations, photography, and other event or wedding typical needs. However, all catering must go through the resort (no outside catering permitted). Lastly, the resort stocks several choices of decorations, table arrangements, and centerpieces. These range from professional, simple, themed, and luxurious.

- **Indigo5** and the **Silver Moon Lounge**, a world-class restaurant and lounge that is overseen by the well-known Chef Robin Sanchez. The cuisine is balanced and modern. From steaks to pasta to local southwestern meals, Indigo5 attracts local patrons in addition to resort guests. While the catering function is separate from the restaurant—though menu items may be shared—the restaurant does support all room service for the resort. The resort also has smaller food venues onsite such as the Terra Cotta Brew coffee shop in the lobby.

Currently, these areas are using Office to various degrees. In some areas, paper and pencil are still used for most business functions. Others have been lucky enough to have some technology savvy team members start Microsoft Office Solutions.

Using your skills, I am confident that you can help us integrate and use Microsoft Office on a whole new level! I hope you are excited to call Painted Paradise Resort & Spa **Your Office**.

Looking forward to working with you more closely!

Aidan Matthews
Aidan Matthews
Chief Technology Officer

Examining Business Model Classifications

| **ADVANCED PROBLEM SOLVING CASES FOR MICROSOFT OFFICE 2016**

REQUIRED SKILLS

1. Work with tables in Datasheet view
2. Create queries that include aggregate functions and calculated fields
3. Maintain records in forms
4. Customize forms
5. Use the Report Wizard
6. Customize a report

Business Dilemma

Using E-Commerce to Manage Employee Schedules and Training

Production & Operations

The Painted Paradise Resort & Spa needs to develop an easier way to manage employee schedules and training throughout the resort and spa. Currently, each manager creates the schedule for their respective department. Unfortunately, this can be very time-consuming as they have to manually determine which employee can work at what times along with how many hours they can work per week and then schedule each employee appropriately. Additionally, a number of employees are trained to work in different departments of the resort and spa and department managers have a difficult time knowing when they may be scheduled already and what training they have completed, which can create challenges in scheduling. The human resources manager believes that the department managers could combine efforts and work with each other along with human resources to ensure that the scheduling process becomes more efficient. You have been asked to enhance the database that will help the department managers manage the schedules. Furthermore, the system will give accounts payable access to the system so they can monitor how much is being spent on payroll each week. Finally, the external vendors that train the resort and spa's employees will need to be able to track training programs and courses that the employees have completed and generate invoices in order to obtain payment for completed training sessions.

Once the database is completed, IT will create a website that allows users to work with the data in the database through the use of an Internet browser. Department managers, human resources employees, accounts payable employees, and the external vendors will be given appropriate access to needed data, creating a business-to-business (B2B) business model.

Files provided by the business:

 ac01Employees.accdb   ac01Training.xlsx

ac01Logo.jpg

Deliverable files:

ac01Employees_LastFirst.accdb   ac01Presentation_LastFirst.pptx

 ac01Analysis_LastFirst.docx   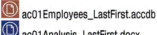 ac01Video_LastFirst

ac01Memo_LastFirst.docx

"It is very important for a database's design to be straightforward and easy to navigate and use. Users need to be able to manipulate data and create useful reports for decision making."

—Jennifer Gren, Database Administrator

Supporting Information

Understanding Business Models

When a business is started, the business inherently runs on a business model even if the business founder never explicitly thought about the model. An organization's **business model** describes the way the business captures value. The model describes the creation, delivery, and retention of value.

The Most Common Business Models

With so many people online using social media and being targeted by online businesses, e-commerce continues to explode and create new business models, such as crowdsourcing and microfinancing. Brick-and-mortar companies have a physical location, such as a grocery or pet store. Some companies are closing their brick-and-mortar stores and focusing on maintaining only an online presence. Other companies that would have started with a brick-and-mortar store in the past are bypassing that option and opening online exclusively. Yet, others use a blended presence of both online and brick-and-mortar. Similar to this, a business may also blend multiple business models in a single business.

While there are many models that separate into providers or producers and consumers or clients, the four most common models are business-to-business (B2B), business-to-consumer (B2C), consumer-to-business (C2B), and consumer-to-consumer (C2C).

Business-to-business (B2B) describes commerce transactions where businesses are doing business directly with other businesses, such as between a manufacturer and a supplier or between a vendor and a retailer. Through the use of B2B, businesses can more efficiently manage their inventories and ordering process by directly contacting each other. Consider what Walmart does to manage its inventory. If a vendor wants Walmart to carry its product in Walmart's stores, then it first needs to purchase a system that integrates with Walmart's inventory replenishment system. One of the many reasons Walmart is able to offer low prices to its customers and maintain a constant level of inventory is due to its renowned inventory replenishment system. Inventory replenishment is triggered by point-of-sale purchases and has become the best in the industry.

Business-to-consumer (B2C) describes commerce transactions between businesses and consumers. This classification is the one that is most talked about, yet the overall volume of B2B transactions is much higher than the volume of B2C transactions. The principal reason for this is that in a typical supply chain there will be many B2B transactions involving raw materials and only one B2C transaction, specifically, the sale of the finished product to the end user. B2C businesses offer products or services directly to consumers. This enables a larger market share and fewer brick-and-mortar establishments. Examples of B2C include Amazon.com, Walmart.com, and McDonalds.com.

Consumer-to-business (C2B) describes commerce transactions between consumers and businesses. Through the use of C2B, consumers offer products or services directly to businesses. This allows individuals to conduct business with anyone, including businesses, through blogs, advertising, and other websites. Because the cost of technology has decreased tremendously, consumers now have access to technologies that they previously could not afford. Examples of C2B include selling textbooks back to the bookstore or paying for advertisement space on a consumer website such as Google or Bing.

Consumer-to-consumer (C2C) describes electronically enabled transactions between consumers through a third party, and these sites exist simply to connect the consumers. A common example is the online auction, such as eBay, where a consumer posts an item for sale and other consumers bid to purchase it.

> **S_S CONSIDER THIS** | **Which Business Model Is eBay?**
>
> Most people only consider eBay as a C2C website. However, it is all four business models wrapped into one. How could eBay also be considered B2B, B2C, and C2B?

Another popular area for C2C is online classified advertising sites, such as Craigslist and Gumtree. Even major online retailers like Amazon allow individuals to sell products through their websites. In this classification, the third party generally charges either a flat fee or commission.

QUICK REFERENCE	Other Business Model Examples

- Bricks-and-clicks: Also known as "click-and-mortar," this is when an organization creates both a physical (bricks) and online (clicks) presence. For example, Walmart and JC Penney both have physical stores where customers can shop. However, customers can also order items online and either pick up their order directly at a local store or have it delivered to their home.
- Build to order: Manufacturers, such as Dell, will use this model not only to sell goods or services, but also to offer the capability to order customized products. The customized product is then assembled to the customer's specifications and shipped to the customer. This provides added value to consumers and allows the manufacturer to only create products that will be sold.
- Microfinancing: A term used to describe financial services delivered to low-income individuals or to those who do not have access to typical banking services. Kiva.org attempts to alleviate poverty by utilizing the Internet and a worldwide network of microfinance institutions.
- Crowdsourcing: The practice of getting work or funding, usually online, from a crowd of people. For example, Wikipedia could have hired a staff to create the online resource; instead, they gave a crowd the ability to create the information on their own.
- Razor-and-blades: Also known as freebie marketing, this occurs when an organization gives away an item in order to generate a continuous revenue stream. For example, when King Camp Gillette first invented the razor, he sold razors at an exaggeratedly low price to create the market for the blades.

Managing Inventory Using E-Commerce

When starting a new business, a database is usually one of the first things to be created. The model that a business uses influences the type of database, the type of interface, and the database design. This will allow data to be stored and retrieved as needed. Think about when you purchase an item online. After you place items in the cart and proceed to check out, you are asked to log in and complete an online form that will allow the company to process the sale. Where does that data go after you press *Complete Order*? Companies store the data in a database for two purposes. First, companies need that data to complete the sale. Second, they use the data to create reports about their business, such as sales and customers.

Business Background

Management at the Painted Paradise Resort & Spa has provided you with a scaled-down version of the database that is currently being used to manage employees, their work availability, and the training they have completed. The database contains the data needed to centralize the scheduling process for departments such as Indigo5, Silver Moon Lounge, Terra Cotta Brew, and Event Planning & Catering. The tables included in the database are as follows.

- tblEmployees: Used to track all employees.
- tblDepartments: Used to track the resort and spa's departments.
- tblTraining: Used to track specific training programs.
- tblEmployeeTraining: Used to track which employees attended which training seminar.
- tblEmployeeDepartment: Used to track which employees can work in which department.
- tblAvailability: Used to track employee availability.
- tblVendors: Used to track the vendors.

Points of Concern

Although tables with data are included in the database, the database's design needs to be modified so it is more appealing and easier to use. Users also need to be able to manipulate the data as well as create useful reports for decision making. For example, you will need to create a report of all the vendors and each of the training seminars they facilitate. Think about how this will change the organization of the database and its interface.

Business Requirements

The human resources manager has been storing training sessions in an Excel workbook and needs you to create a table that will allow the vendors to track sessions offered and the sessions that employees have attended in the database. Use Table 1 to include the following fields, data types, and descriptions. Additionally, determine and create appropriate field properties. Once the table has been created, create appropriate relationships and then import the transaction data from Excel into the tblTraining table.

Field Name	Data Type	Description
SessionID	AutoNumber	This is the training session ID (primary key).
VendorID	Number	This is the vendor ID from the tblVendors table (foreign key).
SessionType	Short Text	This is the type of session; such as Orientation or Customer Service.
DateOffered	Date/Time	This is the date the session was offered.
TimeOffered	Date/Time	This is the time the session was offered.
DepartmentID	Short Text	This is the department ID from the tbl Departments table (foreign key).
SessionFee	Currency	This is the per person charge for attending.

Table 1 Training Sessions

The human resources manager believes it would be a good idea to change the format of the tables that will be used by both its vendors and resort and spa managers.

This will make the data easier to view and edit. Change the tblEmployees, tblDepartments, and tblAvailability tables to have a larger font and alternating row colors. To maintain consistency within the database, the same font size and color should be used for all three tables.

In order to facilitate B2B, several queries will be needed. When creating queries, contemplate who would use them. Would it be the vendors, the resort and spa managers, the human resources manager, accounts payable employees, or everyone? How would the users determine the fields that are included? Additionally, consider if sorting the data in a particular order will make it easier for users to read the query results.

Management needs some queries that will help it monitor key information. First, management needs a query that shows when each employee is available to work. Consider the tables and fields that would provide a complete list of the employees' names along with their availability. Second, management needs a query that shows each department and the employees that are trained to work in each department. Finally, management needs a query that lists all of the vendors and the training sessions they facilitate.

The accounts payable clerks also need several queries that will help them manage the resort and spa's biweekly payroll as well as assist them and the vendors in tracking training session fees. First, the clerks need a query that shows all employees who participated in the Event Service training seminar, one of the most expensive seminars that is offered. Second, the clerks need a query that calculates the total fees due by training session and vendor. Finally, the clerks need an aggregate query that shows the total due, average due, minimum due, and maximum due of the total fees for each training session.

Some users will need a form with a subform that will allow users to view each employee and the departments where they are trained to work. In order for it to be visually appealing and easy for the users to work with, consider applying an appropriate title, as well as changing font sizes and weight, deleting labels, moving controls, and inserting the resort and spa's logo. Using the form, add Silver Moon Lounge to Sigourney Terry's Department list and then add the following new employee.

- First Name: Allie
- Last Name: Massart
- Address: 24 Desert Avenue
- City: Santa Fe
- State: NM
- Phone: (505) 555-8666
- Email Address: amassart@paintedparadise.com
- Job Title: Server
- Hire Date: 1/18/2017
- Department: Event Planning

Users will also need some reports for decision making. In order for the reports to be visually appealing and easy to read, consider applying appropriate titles, changing font sizes and weight, resizing controls, applying conditional formatting, inserting the resort and spa's logo, and saving them as a PDF document. First, users need a report that lists the vendors and their contact information. Second, users need a report that displays each employee's availability. Finally, management would also like reports generated from two of the queries you previously created.

MANAGER'S EMPHASIS
Facilitating B2B

"It is very important for a database's design to be straightforward and easy to navigate and use. Users need to be able to manipulate data and create useful reports for decision making."

Employee database (ac01Employees.accdb)	A snapshot of the employee database. Once you complete the database, IT personnel will implement it.
Training workbook (ac01Training.xlsx)	An Excel workbook that currently houses the different training sessions facilitated by the vendors.
Logo (ac01Logo.jpg)	Painted Paradise Resort & Spa's logo, which can be used on reports and forms.

Analysis Questions

1. How will the queries that were created for management help it monitor key information? How would the business benefit from management being able to retrieve the key information on a regular basis?
2. How many of the current vendors do not provide training sessions to the resort and spa? How could the human resources manager use this information?
3. How could the form benefit users? What other forms could be added to the database that would make it easier for users? How would it help them work with the data?
4. What type of decisions could be made by using the reports? Who would be able to benefit from using the reports?
5. What would be the easiest way for all users to access the database and work with the data?
6. How did the B2B aspect of the business models influence your decisions?
7. How does the B2B aspect influence how the business interacts with the other businesses in your solution?
8. Do you have any recommendations for future changes to the system that would better suit the B2B model?

Deliverables

1. Submit the ac01Employees_LastFirst.accdb database as directed by your instructor.
2. As directed by your instructor, submit the following.

   ac01Analysis_LastFirst.docx with your answers to the analysis questions.

   ac01Memo_LastFirst.docx to explain and document your solution.

   ac01Presentation_LastFirst.pptx to present your recommendations, concerns, and findings to the analysis questions.

   Post a video presentation to YouTube or other instructor-provided location with a duration of less than five minutes.

Checklist

☐ The tblTraining table is created and includes appropriate formatting.

☐ The tblEmployees, tblDepartments, and tblAvailability tables are formatted correctly.

☐ All queries needed for management are created and formatted appropriately.

☐ All queries needed for accounts payable are created and formatted appropriately.

☐ The user form with a subform is created and formatted appropriately.

☐ Silver Moon Lounge is added to Sigourney Terry's Department list by using the form.

☐ A new record for Allie Massart is entered by using the form.

☐ All reports are created and formatted appropriately.

☐ All analysis questions are answered thoroughly.

☐ The memo thoroughly explains and documents the solution.

☐ The PowerPoint presentation thoroughly presents recommendations, concerns, and findings to the analysis questions, including appropriate formatting.

☐ The YouTube video includes all required steps including appropriate formatting.

☐ All deliverables are completed and named correctly.

Key Terms

Business-to-business 2
Business-to-consumer 2

Business model 2
Consumer-to-business 2

Consumer-to-consumer 3

Systems Development Life Cycle Basics and Determining Business Requirements

| ADVANCED PROBLEM SOLVING CASES FOR MICROSOFT OFFICE 2016

REQUIRED SKILLS

1. Control the way data is entered with data validation rules, lookup fields, and input masks

2. Apply advanced data type properties to fields

3. Use the Table Analyzer Wizard to ensure tables are normalized

4. Create queries with the "most" values

5. Create queries that use wildcard characters, advanced operators, and parameters

6. Create queries that use the Concatenate, IIf, IsNull, Date, and Round functions

Business Dilemma

Production & Operations

Developing a Phone App to Help Manage Housekeepers

The Painted Paradise Resort & Spa managers need to develop an easier way to manage how housekeepers currently clean rooms and keep track of those that are cleaned. As of now, housekeepers walk from room to room and manually keep track of which rooms need what services and items in a notebook that is provided to them by their supervisor. Unfortunately, some employees forget to write down some details or specify if a room needs to be visited at another time—if the room is still occupied or there is a "Do not disturb" sign on the door handle. Additionally, other housekeepers will not be aware of their colleagues' needs, which creates many inefficiencies throughout the hotel.

Management believes that they could develop a more efficient method of managing the housekeeping process with a phone app. The IT department along with management have developed a database with some sample data that will be used to track reservations, when rooms are serviced, and what items—such as shampoo, tissues, and soap—were distributed. Some employees have started designing the phone app using the systems development life cycle (SDLC). The database tables need to be modified and queries need to be created for data analysis.

Files provided by the business:

 ac02Housekeeping.accdb   ac02OrganizationalChart.docx

ac02BusinessProcesses.pdf   ac02JobDescriptions.txt

Deliverable files:

 ac02Housekeeping_LastFirst.accdb   ac02Presentation_LastFirst.pptx

ac02Analysis_LastFirst.docx   ac02Video_LastFirst

ac02Memo_LastFirst.docx

Supporting Information

Understanding the Systems Development Life Cycle

When a system is developed, information systems professionals follow a proven methodology called the systems development life cycle (SDLC). The **systems development life cycle** is composed of five phases that systems engineers and developers use to plan for, design, build, test, and implement information systems.

Generally, employees drive the decision to build new information systems when they are having difficulty performing their jobs. For example, a payroll clerk who uses an accounting information system every day will easily be able to discern what needs to be improved within that system or when it is time for a new system.

Phases of the SDLC

The phases of the SDLC are essential for developers—planning, analysis, design, implementation, and support (see Figure 1). The SDLC, also known as the **waterfall method**, contains a sequence of steps in which the output of each step becomes the input for the next step. The SDLC is referred to as a life cycle because it starts with a business need, proceeds to a valuation of the functions a system must have to fulfill the need, and ends when the benefits of the system no longer offset the maintenance costs.

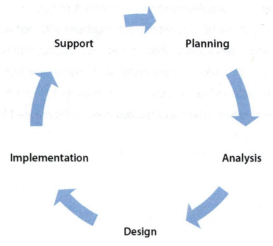

Figure 1   Five phases of the systems development life cycle

The Planning Phase

The first phase of the SDLC is the **planning phase**, the most important phase of any systems development project regardless of whether the system being developed is a simple database used to track golfers and tee times, a phone app, or even a system that integrates several functional areas in an organization. IT professionals, along with their colleagues, must carefully plan the activities needed for the project's success.

In the planning phase, three primary activities are conducted: Identify and select the system for development, conduct feasibility studies, and develop the project plan. One of the primary activities accomplished during this phase is determining which systems will help an organization achieve its strategic goals. To determine which system will be developed, an organization documents all proposed systems and prioritizes them by critical success factors. A **critical success factor** (CSF) is a factor that is critical to an organization's success and allows the business to rank which problems require immediate attention.

A **feasibility study** determines if the proposed solution is feasible from a financial, technical, and organizational standpoint. Organizations want to ensure that benefits of the project outweigh the costs by performing a **cost-benefit analysis**. Additionally, they need to determine if the project will meet its desired objectives, if the project timeline is realistic, and that they have the technical skills needed to build the system.

Finally, the project plan needs to be developed, which includes specifying when deliverables are due. If deadlines are missed, the project plan will need to be updated to reflect this as well as push back due dates of items that follow the missed deadline.

The Analysis Phase

The second phase of the SDLC is the **analysis phase**, which includes gathering business requirements, creating business process diagrams, and performing a buy versus build analysis. **Business requirements**, which are probably the most essential element of the analysis phase, specify the business needs that the new system must include in order for it to be successful. When determining business requirements, it is important to obtain input from end users. For example, a business requirement might specify that the system must track all employees by department, position, and length of employment. This requirement states what the system needs to do from a business perspective, but not how the system is specifically going to accomplish this.

Once the business requirements are determined, the systems analyst investigates how the organization performs specific tasks or business processes. A **business process** is a series of steps taken to accomplish a specific goal. For example, think about the steps that a payroll clerk needs to take to calculate the weekly payroll for hourly employees. Calculating payroll is a business process that requires several steps, including the following.

- Is the employee a salaried or hourly employee?
- If hourly, how many hours were worked during the week?
- Did the employee work over 40 hours?
- Calculate the gross pay. If the employee worked under 40 hours, multiply the hours worked by the hourly rate. If the employee worked over 40 hours, subtract 40 from the hours worked to determine the amount of overtime the employee will be paid. Multiply 40 by the hourly rate, multiply the difference between the hours worked and 40 by 1.5 times the employee's salary, and then add the numbers together.
- Subtract taxes and other deductions as necessary.

Known as **process modeling**, diagrams are then created to illustrate the processes such as calculating payroll. The most common process model is a **data flow diagram** (DFD), which maps the flow of data within the organization and its functional areas along with the data stores contained in the system. Once the process models are created, the organization needs to determine which option is more practical—buying or building a new system.

After collecting pertinent information, and prior to moving forward with the development process, an organization needs to determine if it benefits them to build the system as opposed to buying a system. Remember the saying, "Don't reinvent the wheel." The rule of thumb is to always research if a system that will meet the needs of the organization exists in the marketplace. Purchasing ready-made software can lead to a higher return on investment because developing a system from scratch takes a great deal of time and effort.

The Design Phase

The third phase is the **design phase**. The design phase is where the information collected throughout the previous phases is used in developing the system and the infrastructure that will be needed to support the system. Additionally, testing should occur in this phase. A typical systems development effort has hundreds or thousands of test conditions. Every single test condition must be executed to verify that the system performs as expected. If bugs are found, they must be fixed prior to proceeding to the fourth phase.

 CONSIDER THIS | **What Would Happen?**

Think about what would happen if testing was not performed. How would employees react to an unstable system? Finding bugs? Would they be very eager to use the system if they continued to have problems with it?

The Implementation Phase

The fourth phase is the **implementation phase**, which involves training and conversion. Training is determined by the conversion method that is chosen. For example, if a phased conversion is selected, then training can be offered at scheduled intervals as the new system is rolled out. However, if a cold turkey conversion is selected, then all training must take place prior to the system's roll out.

The Support Phase

The fifth phase is the **support phase**, which includes help desk support, maintenance, and system modifications. Many believe that the support phase only involves correcting problems. While this is part of the support phase, this phase comprises carrying out changes, corrections, additions, and upgrades to ensure that the system continues to meet the business goals. The support phase is the longest phase and continues for the life of the system. Once it becomes financially ineffective to support the system, it is time to progress back to the planning phase. It is important for the organization to have a system that will assist in moving it toward achieving its strategic goals.

Developing a Phone App

When an organization develops an app, that app needs to integrate with its database. For example, the hotel will need to store reservations—primarily to see when rooms are occupied and guests check out—regardless of whether those reservations are entered via the app or via the database by an employee.

Business Background

April Meyer, Internal Software Systems Manager at the Painted Paradise Resort & Spa, has provided you with the ac02Housekeeping database that will be used to manage housekeepers and the work they perform as well as guest information and activity. The database contains the data needed to centralize the housekeeping scheduling process at the hotel. The tables included in the database are as follows.

- tblChargeDetails: Used to track what specific item or service was charged to the guest's room
- tblEmployees: Used to track hotel employees
- tblEmployeeService: Used to track when rooms were serviced and by whom
- tblGuests: Used to track guests
- tblPayments: Used to track the payment that a guest makes toward their bill
- tblReservations: Used to track guest reservations and what room they will be occupying
- tblRoomCharges: Used to track when guests charge items to their room
- tblRooms: Used to track the rooms at the hotel
- tblService: Used to track the cleaning schedule

Points of Concern

Although tables and data are included in the database, some need to be modified so they are more functional. Additionally, useful queries need to be created for decision making. For example, you will need to create a query for who cleaned each room and when each room was cleaned. Think about how this will affect the app's usefulness.

Business Requirements

The IT department believes that developing an app is a great idea for the hotel. The database contains sample data that will be integrated with the app once it is fully functional and implemented. April has asked you to make some modifications to the format of the tblEmployees table so it is easier to enter and manage data. Open the tblEmployees table in Design view. Modify field properties, such as field sizes, input masks, and captions, and add validation rules and validation text to ensure there is consistency in entering data. Additionally, add fields with appropriate properties that will allow you to track the following.

- Employees who have downloaded the app, indicated by having a user name and password.
- Whether a service was scheduled through the app, via phone, or in person.

Once the field properties have been modified and the new fields have been added, enter sample data to test all changes. Next, use the ac02OrganizationalChart.docx file to help modify the tblEmployees table and create the tblJobDescriptions table. For the tblEmployees table, consider adding fields such as annual salary if they are a full-time employee, the date of hire, an employee photo, and if they are a Certified Executive Housekeeper (CEH). Use the ac02JobDescriptions.txt file to help create the tblJobDescriptions table and then import the data into the tblJobDescriptions table. Ensure all necessary properties are added in the two tables. Finally, analyze the tblEmployees table to ensure that it is normalized. Make all necessary changes to tables and relationships.

In order for the database to be useful, several queries will be needed. When creating queries, anticipate who would use them. Would it be the guests, hotel management, housekeeping and other employees, or everyone? How would the users determine the fields that are included? Additionally, consider if sorting the data in a particular order or adding parameters will make it easier for users to read the query results.

Management needs several queries that will help them manage the housekeepers. First, based on a biweekly pay period, management needs a query that calculates the employees' gross income, rounded off to the nearest dollar. Second, management needs to allocate enough funds in the budget for cost of living increases of 2% in employee salaries. Thus, they need a query that calculates employees' salaries including the increase along with the difference between the total increase and total current salaries. Third, management needs a query that calculates the total months and the total years that each employee has worked at the hotel. Next, management needs a query that concatenates the employees' first and last name fields along with their job title that they can use when name badges need to be ordered. Additionally, management needs a query that lists all employees who began employment at the hotel within a specific time frame, where the criteria are entered when the query runs. Furthermore, management wants to see the rooms that were cleaned each day and by which housekeeper so they can measure the efficiency of each housekeeper. Finally, management needs a query that lists all employees who are CEH certified.

MANAGER'S
EMPHASIS
When creating queries, consider formatting fields to ensure the data displays as expected such as currency and percentage.

Debbie Burgess, Housekeeping Manager, also needs a few queries that will help her manage the housekeeping process. First, to encourage employees to use the phone app, the hotel will offer a $50 bonus to housekeepers who consistently use the app. Each time they use the app to log when a service is complete, they will receive one entry into a drawing for a $50 bonus. Additionally, Debbie would like a listing of all housekeepers, their email address, and username. If they do not have a username, then have the field display "Not downloaded yet." Finally, she needs a query that calculates how many times each employee used the app on a specific day. She also wants to be able to enter a specific date when the query runs. After all database objects have been modified or created, use the To-Be business process diagram to ensure that the database will be able to track all data associated with the app.

Provided Files

Housekeeping database (ac02Housekeeping.accdb)	A snapshot of the hotel's database. Once you complete the database, the IT department will implement it.
As-Is business process diagram (ac02BusinessProcesses.pdf)	Illustrates the current process of scheduling housekeeping.
To-Be business process diagram (ac02BusinessProcesses.pdf)	Illustrates how scheduling housekeeping will be accomplished within the phone app.
Organizational chart (ac02OrganizationalChart.docx)	Illustrates the structure of the hotel.
Job descriptions (ac02JobDescriptions.txt)	Lists the details of each job description.

Analysis Questions

1. How will the queries that were created for management help them manage employees?
2. Explain how the process of analyzing the tblEmployees table changed your database.
3. How could the database benefit app users? What other objects could be added to the database that would make it easier to interact with the app?
4. When performing a buy versus build analysis, how can purchasing ready-made software lead to a higher return on the investment?
5. What type of decisions could be made by viewing the queries? Who would be able to benefit from using these queries?
6. What would be the best implementation strategy for the database and app? Why?
7. How did the To-Be business process diagram influence your decisions?
8. How does the SDLC influence how the IT department interacts with employees in other functional areas?
9. Do you have any recommendations for future changes to the system that would make it easier for employees to use?

Deliverables

1. Submit the ac02Housekeeping_LastFirst.accdb database as directed by your instructor.
2. As directed by your instructor, submit the following.

   ac02Analysis_LastFirst.docx with your answers to the analysis questions.

   ac02Memo_LastFirst.docx to explain and document your solution.

   ac02Presentation_LastFirst.pptx to present your recommendations, concerns, and findings to the analysis questions.

   Post a video presentation to YouTube or other instructor-provided location with a duration of less than five minutes.

Checklist

☐ The field properties in all tables are modified and include appropriate formatting.

☐ The tblEmployee and tblJobDescriptions tables are created and include appropriate formatting.

☐ The tblEmployees table is normalized.

☐ All queries needed for management are created and formatted appropriately.

☐ All queries needed for the housekeeping manager are created and formatted appropriately.

☐ All analysis questions are answered thoroughly.

☐ The memo thoroughly explains and documents the solution.

☐ The PowerPoint presentation thoroughly presented recommendations, concerns, and findings to the analysis questions, including appropriate formatting.

☐ The YouTube video includes all required steps including appropriate formatting.

☐ All deliverables are completed and named correctly.

Key Terms

Analysis phase   11
Business process   11
Business requirement   11
Cost-benefit analysis   11
Critical success factor   11

Data flow diagram   11
Design phase   12
Feasibility study   11
Implementation phase   12
Planning phase   10

Process modeling   11
Support phase   13
Systems development
   life cycle   10
Waterfall method   10

Anticipating and Answering Business Questions with Advanced Queries

Access Case 3	ADVANCED PROBLEM SOLVING CASES FOR MICROSOFT OFFICE 2016

REQUIRED SKILLS

1. Create aggregate queries
2. Create subqueries with business calculations
3. Use the Crosstab Query Wizard
4. Create a new table using a make table query
5. Work with update queries
6. Create inner and outer joins
7. Use the Find Unmatched Query Wizard

Business Dilemma

Answering Managerial Questions at Collegiate Book Rentals

Production & Operations

Collegiate Book Rentals is an up-and-coming business in the college book rental market. It has been renting textbooks for two years and would like to grow its business in the next two to five years. Jasmine has been keeping track of rentals in an Excel spreadsheet and has started to keep track of some titles in an Access database. She would like to eventually move all the data into Access, but first, she needs to show management how powerful Access can be. She knows how to create basic queries, but the questions management has been asking her to answer are beyond her comfort level. She needs some assistance creating queries that will answer some of management's specific questions.

MANAGER'S ADVICE ON THIS CASE

"The calculations in Access often take multiple queries, or subqueries, to get to the final result. While this in itself is not a problem, I am concerned about the number of queries that will appear in the Navigation Pane and trying to determine which query to run for the correct result. Therefore, it is critical that the queries be named in such a way that they are easy to identify."

—Kay Fultz, Controller

File provided by the business:

 ac03BookRental.accdb

Deliverable files:

 ac03BookRental_LastFirst.accdb   ac03Presentation_LastFirst.pptx

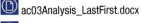 ac03Analysis_LastFirst.docx    ac03Video_LastFirst

ac03Memo_LastFirst.docx

Using Advanced Queries to Provide Business Information

Managers use summarized data to make business decisions every day. In Access, simple queries summarize data row by row, which is often adequate but does not always provide the answers being sought. Decisions regarding inventory, advertising, personnel, and production often require data to be summarized as well as calculations to be performed, such as a count of employees or the total revenue. Advanced queries can provide these types of results from data stored in tables as well as from results of queries. Understanding how to group data and use aggregate functions, subqueries, query wizards, and action queries provides the user with powerful decision-making tools in Access that can enhance the decision-making process.

 CONSIDER THIS | **Access or Excel?**

Many people use Excel for all data analysis because they are unfamiliar with or intimidated by Access. Why do you think people are so reluctant to learn Access? What aspects of it appear to be the most intimidating? Is showing someone what Access can do the best way to convince him or her to learn Access? What else could you do?

Grouping Data with Aggregate Queries

Often data in a table is made up of recurring transactions such as pay records, item sales, or inventory purchases. In order to group data to summarize the total amount paid to an employee, or the total number of items sold, or the total cost of inventory purchases, an aggregate query can be used. By using the **Group By aggregate function**, a user can not only group data to summarize multiple records in a table, but also specify criteria and perform calculations on that grouped data.

The Group By aggregate function specifies on which field the grouping will occur. By adding a **Where aggregate function**, specific criteria can be added to the summarized data without grouping the data in that particular field. For example, the total amount paid to an employee for a specific time period can be calculated. In this case, the Where criteria would be the time period requested, while the aggregate function for the amount paid would be Sum, and the Group By would be the employee name or ID. By adding an **Expression aggregate function**, a calculation can be performed on the summarized data. Total revenue, total sales, and counts of records are just a few of the calculations that can be performed in an aggregate query.

Creating Subqueries

While an aggregate query may provide results such as total revenues or total sales, more sophisticated queries can build on this information and provide calculations like percent of total revenues or percent of total sales. These types of queries often build on existing query data sets rather than table data sets.

A **subquery** is a select query that is nested inside of another select query. You use a subquery when you want to create a query from previously queried data. For example, one query might calculate total revenues, and another will use the results of that query to calculate percent of total revenues.

Using the Query Wizards for Advanced Queries

A **crosstab query** is different than aggregate functions because it groups the aggregates by the column and row headings. The added value in decision making is that the crosstab queries are useful for summarizing data, calculating statistics, identifying bad data, and looking for trends. Crosstab queries are also a useful way to present data in a compact and summarized form. Crosstab queries use aggregate functions and then group the results by two sets of values—one down the side of the datasheet as rows and the other across the top as columns—and transform rows of data to columns. The **Crosstab Query Wizard** prompts you to choose which field will be used as the row headings (up to three), which fields' values will be used as the column headings, and which fields contain values to summarize.

The **Find Unmatched Query Wizard** finds records in one table that do not have related records in another table. This type of query can be very helpful when you want to find customers in one table without orders or appointments in another table. These unmatched customers can then be targeted for additional marketing of your goods or services. The Find Unmatched Query Wizard is also helpful to cleanse data in a table. If you wanted to discontinue items based on ones that are not selling, you can find those records easily using the wizard.

While it may seem quicker to create expressions and calculations in Excel, often transferring the data to Access and creating the expressions as part of queries is quicker. This is especially true if the data comes as a different workbook each month and the same analysis needs to be done with the data. If the data can be brought into Access, then the queries can be run each month on the new data without having to recreate the calculations. The time taken up front to create the queries will be well worth the effort each time new data is run through the database.

Using Action Queries in a Database

While select queries are used to display and manipulate data but not actually change the data, an action query is a query that makes changes to records or moves records from one table to another. Action queries are used to change data in existing tables or make new tables based on a query's data set.

There are four different types of action queries: **make table query**, **append query**, **update query**, and **delete query**. It is important to remember that these action queries permanently modify the data in tables, and since there is no undo feature for action queries, you should be cautious when running them. It is a good business practice to create a backup of your database before you run any action query in case you need to restore any of the changed data.

Anticipating and Answering Business Questions with Advanced Queries

While Excel is an excellent program in which to collect data, Access has some powerful query tools that are just not available in Excel. Often, the questions managers want answered can be more easily answered using advanced queries in Access, even to the extent of calculating revenues, percent of revenues, and other more complex expressions.

Business Background

Jasmine has been keeping track of the company's book rentals in Excel, but the file is getting too large, and some of the questions management has been asking cannot be easily answered with the data in its current Excel format. Jasmine needs to use the Access database she has started to answer some of management's questions in order to convince them to move all their records to Access from Excel. She has given you a database to work with that contains some old data. The database includes the following tables:

- tblBooks: Used to track each book's information.
- tblContracts: Used to show information about the company's current contracts for book rentals.
- tblCustomers: Used to track customer information.
- tblUpdatedBooks: Contains the new 13-digit ISBNs for books in tblBooks.

Information on books includes the Book ID, ISBN, Title, Publisher, Edition, Subject, Condition, Copyright, and Monthly Rental amount.

Contract information includes the Contract ID, Customer ID, Book, Rental Date, and the number of months the book is being rented. Books may be rented for 3, 6, 9, or 12 months.

Customer information includes Customer ID, First and Last Name, Address, City, State, Zip Code, and Phone.

Points of Concern

Some queries, such as action queries, make permanent changes to data in the database. It is always a good business practice to back up your database before running any action queries so that if data is accidentally changed, it can be restored with the backup.

Business Requirements

Jasmine believes the Access database will better serve the needs of management when it comes to analyzing and understanding the data that is being accumulated. Using advanced queries, including aggregate queries, subqueries, query wizards, and action queries, you must create queries that will answer the following questions management has asked:

- By subject, how many books have been rented so far?
- By title, how many books have been rented? All titles should be listed, even ones with no rentals.
- By title, how many books have been rented for a 9-month period?
- By title, how many books have been rented for each time period (3, 6, 9, and 12 months)? The results should be in one query.
- What is the total revenue, by subject?
- What is the total revenue for all book rentals?
- How much does each subject contribute to total revenue?
- Which titles are not currently being rented?
- What is the end date for each of the current contracts? Create a query to calculate the end date and then make a new table from the query results. The new table should have all the functionality and properties of the tblContracts table.
- The tblBooks table needs to be updated with the 13-digit ISBN, which can be found in tblUpdatedBooks. The ISBN should be reformatted in tblBooks after the update.

There should be at least one query to answer each of the above questions, although some may require multiple queries to attain the final answer. Jasmine would like you to make sure that all field names are changed as necessary, field columns are resized, and the overall look of every query is professional.

In addition to the above queries, create three more queries that might help Jasmine answer different questions that management might have. These queries should be aggregate queries, queries using a Wizard, or subqueries without using an action query. Use the Description property for each query to explain, in one or two sentences, what the query is doing by right-clicking the query and selecting Object Properties.

Provided File

Book rental database (ac03BookRental.accdb)	The book rental database with only tables.

Analysis Questions

1. Discuss some of the calculations that can be created using aggregate queries. What kinds of decisions can these calculations help managers make?
2. How can you calculate expressions when the data is not immediately available in a table? What is this called, and how did you use this technique to answer the manager's questions for Jasmine?
3. What is the difference between an action query and a select query? When you are working with action queries, why is it important to create a backup of your database first?
4. Why is it important to keep your database up to date and organized? What type of data might become unneeded or unwanted over time? What type of query can help you clean up your database?

5. When you run a database query to find data in related tables, only records that have matching values on both sides of the relationship are found. Most of the time, this result will be adequate, but other times, you may want to control which records will be displayed. What kind of query allows you to control the records you see, and how did you use this type of query to help answer the manager's questions for Jasmine?

6. What other queries did you create to help Jasmine anticipate her manager's questions? What types of queries were they, and what questions did they answer?

Deliverables

1. Submit the ac03BookRental_LastFirst.accdb database as directed by your instructor.
2. As directed by your instructor, submit the following.

   ac03Analysis_LastFirst.docx with your answers to the analysis questions.

   ac03Memo_LastFirst.docx to explain and document your solution.

   ac03Presentation_LastFirst.pptx to present your recommendations, concerns, and findings to the analysis questions.

   Post a video presentation to YouTube or other instructor-provided location with a duration of less than five minutes.

Checklist

☐ Queries were created to answer management's questions listed in the Business Requirements.

☐ Three additional queries were created to help provide management with additional information that they did not specifically ask for.

☐ All analysis questions are answered thoroughly.

☐ The memo thoroughly explains and documents the solution.

☐ The PowerPoint presentation thoroughly presents recommendations, concerns, and findings to the analysis questions, including appropriate formatting.

☐ The YouTube video includes all required steps including appropriate formatting.

☐ All deliverables are completed and named correctly.

Key Terms

Append query   20
Crosstab query   19
Crosstab Query Wizard   19
Delete query   20
Expression aggregate
   function   18

Find Unmatched Query
   Wizard   19
Group By aggregate
   function   18
Make table query   20
Subquery   19

Update query   20
Where aggregate
   function   18

Increasing Productivity with Forms and Reports

Access Case 4 | ## ADVANCED PROBLEM SOLVING CASES FOR MICROSOFT OFFICE 2016

REQUIRED SKILLS

1. Create a form from multiple tables
2. Modify the form property sheet
3. Modify the form header
4. Modify the form in Design view
5. Create a multipage form using tab controls
6. Create a report
7. Modify the report in Design view
8. Create a parameter report

Business Dilemma

Increasing Productivity with Access Forms and Reports

Production & Operations

CCIB is a small company that works with clients on various technology issues. It sells subscriptions for its services as well as takes appointments for work to be completed offsite at its clients' locations. Josh, the owner of CCIB, has created a database to keep track of the calls it receives, its customers, and its employees. He would like to create forms and reports to be able to manage this data and allow his employees to easily work with the data. Most of his employees are not familiar or comfortable with Access, so he needs the forms and reports to be user-friendly.

MANAGER'S ADVICE ON THIS CASE

"Forms and reports should make using Access easier for users to manipulate the data. Forms should be created with the assumption that the person doing the data entry is not familiar with Access. By making the data entry process easier, the chance of errors will be reduced. We want the data entry process to be simple and fun—not complicated and stressful. Reports will help provide management with the information needed to make better business decisions. Before any reports are created, it will be helpful to meet with management to decide what information is needed and how it should be organized."

—Mitch Jeinks, Controller

Files provided by the business:

 ac04Calls.accdb
 ac04CCIBLogo.jpg

Deliverable files:

 ac04Calls_LastFirst.accdb
 ac04Analysis_LastFirst.docx
 ac04Memo_LastFirst.docx
 ac04Presentation_LastFirst.pptx
 ac04Video_LastFirst

Using Forms and Reports to Increase Productivity

Forms are excellent tools to help improve productivity when working in an Access database. Forms can be used to enter records, edit records, delete records, and display records from either a single Access table or multiple related Access tables. Forms can also be used to look up data in a table, navigate records in a table, open other forms, reports, or queries, and print tables. A well-designed form can make it easy for any user, one familiar with Access or not, to enter and manage data in a database.

Reports can also increase productivity by providing a user with easy-to-read and professional-looking configurations of the data. Reports allow a user to subtotal, total, group, and sort data and present it in a variety of ways depending on the need. While forms are used primarily for managing data, reports are used for printing the data for a wide variety of interested parties.

Designing Professional and Useful Forms

When designing a new form, there are three views you can work with. The **Form view** shows the data in the form and allows you to enter and edit data. You should always refer back to Form view to check how your form is working and to make sure the changes you are making are doing what you want. The **Layout view** is useful to work in to change field sizes and to move fields around since you can see the data while you are making these changes. You can only view the data in this view, but it is helpful to be able to visualize the changes you are making. The **Design view** shows only the form design and not the data, but allows you to make any and all changes to the form. You can change field properties, tab order, and field sizes, as well as add objects such as buttons in Design view.

The **property sheet** allows you to change the characteristics of fields and form parts. **Field properties** include features such as field formatting, background colors, special effects, input masks, validation rules, default values, macro procedures, captions and field names, and many more. The property sheet can be opened in either the Layout view or Design view. By changing these properties, you can make a standard form more professional.

In order to make a form more useful, features like combo boxes and tab controls can be added. Combo boxes allow a user to look up information directly on a form, while tab controls allow you to make a multipage form, giving you more room to add fields.

When a form is going to be used by someone who is unfamiliar with Access or with the specific database, adding buttons and changing the navigation methods can help simplify many tasks. By removing the navigation bar and replacing navigation with buttons, a novice Access user will not have to figure out how to go from one record to the next. Buttons that open and close other tables, queries, forms, or reports also make it possible to hide the Navigation Pane, which can prevent unwanted access to other objects in the database.

One of the first considerations when designing a form is determining who the user will be. How many people will be using the form should also be considered. When a more diverse group of people uses a form, the chances of them not being familiar with it are greater, and therefore, more safeguards should be put into place for accurate data entry. Finally, you should consider how much access you want the user to have to the data and decide which fields they can only see versus which fields they can change. By modifying field and form properties and navigation tools and adding other objects, almost any level of user can be accommodated while also protecting the data.

Designing Professional Reports

The same data represented in different formats can often tell a different story. The goal in designing a report should be to present the data in a way that will be useful and professional looking for its audience.

A report has more views than a form. While the Report view, Layout view, and Design view are similar to the different views for a form, there is also a **Print Preview** that allows the user to see the report as it will print. The Print Preview also allows the user to change print options such as page orientation, size, margins, and other options. When designing a report, it is good practice to periodically switch to Print Preview during the process to see what the report will look like in printed form, since printing is the primary purpose of a report.

Adding totals and subtotals, as well as calculated fields, can add much needed summary options to a report. Sorting and grouping data can present the same data in various ways, depending on the needs of the user.

Increasing Productivity with Forms and Reports

While the basic forms and reports that can be created with the wizards are helpful and often enough to meet a business's needs, sometimes more advanced features can make the forms and reports more user-friendly, especially for users not familiar with Access.

Business Background

Josh Mikum, the owner of CCIB, has created a database to track customer calls, customer contact information, and employee contact information with the following objects:

- tblCalls: Used to track calls received from customers.
- tblCustomers: Used to track customer contact information.
- tblEmployees: Used to track CCIB employee contact information.
- qryEmployeeCallHistory: A parameter query to see what calls are associated with the employee name entered.
- qryCustomerName: Used to combine the customer first and last name in one field.
- qryEmployeeName: Used to combine the employee first and last name in one field.

Points of Concern

The forms and reports that are created for this database must be easy to use, especially for employees who are not familiar with or comfortable using Access. When designing them, and especially the form, you must keep in mind that the user does not necessarily know how a form "works" and assume that what they see is what they get. You should assume the user has no knowledge of Access and the form should be self-explanatory.

Business Requirements

The way the database is designed right now, there is not an effective way to retrieve all the customer information and the call information together in one place. Josh would like to see a form where any one of his employees can easily look up a customer by last name or company name and see not only the contact information, but also the call history for that customer. From this same form, he would like to be able to navigate to other customer records using buttons rather than the navigation bar. This way, even if his employees have never used Access, they would still be comfortable using the form to find a customer, add a customer, or change customer details. He does not, however, want the employees to be able to add or change the call history information.

The features he would like to see on the form include:

- A way to lookup the customer by last name or company name.
- The first name, last name, job title, and company for each customer. These fields can be updated by the user. The ID should also be shown but should only be shown for informational purposes. The user should be prevented from

changing this field by changing how it looks on the form as well as by changing its form properties.

- At least four navigation buttons including Next Customer, Previous Customer, Find Customer, and Add Customer. For users, the buttons should replace the navigation bar for navigating through records.
- Two tabs on the form: one with the contact information for each customer, and one showing the call history for the customer. The properties for the call history detail should be set so the user cannot make changes to this data from the form. The contact information tab should come before the call history tab.
- A calculated field on the main form showing the total calls for the customer. The user should be prevented from editing the data in this field by changing how it looks on the form as well as by changing its form properties.
- The form should look professional with the company logo and appropriate matching background colors.
- The date and time should be anchored in the top-right corner.
- The tab order should go from top to bottom in a logical sequence for the user.

Josh would also like to have a report that is based on the parameter query, qryEmployeeCallHistory. The report should show the Employee name (first and last), Status, Priority, Caller, Call Time, Category, Description, Comments, and Resolved Date. All fields should be wide enough to view the text. The calls for each employee should be grouped by Status so that the total number of calls for each status can be calculated and shown on the report. The status "Active" should stand out in a different font color than the rest of the status options. The logo should be added to the report. A form should be set up so the user can enter an employee's last name and click a button to either run the parameter query, run the report, or close the form.

Provided Files

Calls database (ac04Calls.accdb)	The calls database with only tables and queries.
Logo (ac04CCIBLogo.jpg)	The CCIB logo to use on the customer form and report.

Analysis Questions

1. Why is it important to make a form user-friendly?
2. What characteristics would you give to a user-friendly form? What features can you add and what properties can you change to make a form more user-friendly?
3. What can you do to protect data on a form when you want it to be viewed but not changed? What is the difference between locking and disabling a field, and when would you use each option?
4. Why might you group or sort the same data differently in a report? What advantages does grouping and sorting offer in terms of understating report data?
5. How can giving users control of the data they will see, like in a parameter query or report, be helpful? When can using a parameter query or report not be helpful? Are there times when this might be more of a hindrance than a help to the user?
6. What other types of forms would be helpful for CCIB to create in their database? What other types of reports could they use?

Deliverables

1. Submit the ac04Calls_LastFirst.accdb database as directed by your instructor.
2. As directed by your instructor, submit the following.

   ac04Analysis_LastFirst.docx with your answers to the analysis questions.

   ac04Memo_LastFirst.docx to explain and document your solution.

   ac04Presentation_LastFirst.pptx to present your recommendations, concerns, and findings to the analysis questions.

   Post a video presentation to YouTube or other instructor-provided location with a duration of less than five minutes.

Checklist

☐ A form was created to look up and enter customer data and includes the appropriate navigation buttons.

☐ A report showing the number of calls for each status type was created with appropriate formatting.

☐ A form was created to allow the user to enter an employee's last name and then either run a query, run a report, or close the form.

☐ All analysis questions are answered thoroughly.

☐ The memo thoroughly explains and documents the solution.

☐ The PowerPoint presentation thoroughly presents recommendations, concerns, and findings to the analysis questions, including appropriate formatting.

☐ The YouTube video includes all required steps including appropriate formatting.

☐ All deliverables are completed and named correctly.

Key Terms

Design view   24
Field properties   24

Form view   24
Layout view   24

Print Preview   25
Property sheet   24

Developing a Main User Interface

| ## ADVANCED PROBLEM SOLVING CASES FOR MICROSOFT OFFICE 2016

REQUIRED SKILLS

1. Create select and action queries
2. Incorporate logical functions
3. Create reports
4. Create forms with command buttons
5. Create stand alone, embedded, and AutoExec macros

Business Dilemma

Developing a Payroll System for Bob's Pizzeria

Production & Operations

Bob's Pizzeria is a local pizzeria with a small staff consisting of managers, delivery drivers, and kitchen staff. Currently, the managers keep track of hours worked in a log book. Using this outdated method means that management spends a lot more time processing payroll than is necessary. You have been asked to develop a payroll system for clocking in and out using Microsoft Access. You will create the necessary tables with appropriate relationships established. You will create a user-friendly interface for employees to use to clock in and out. The system will also include access to necessary queries and reports to assist management with processing payroll.

MANAGER'S ADVICE ON THIS CASE

"When developing a user interface for any system, the most important step is gathering the requirements. If the requirements for the users are not met, the system will be considered a failure. Be sure to take the time to understand the requirements before beginning any work."

— Ms. Layla Garcia, CIO

Files provided by the business:

- ac05PayrollInterface.accdb
- ac05BusinessProcessMap.pdf

Deliverable files:

- ac05PayrollInterface_LastFirst.accdb
- ac05LoginData_LastFirst.txt
- ac05Analysis_LastFirst.docx
- ac05Memo_LastFirst.docx
- ac05Presentation_LastFirst.pptx
- ac05Video_LastFirst

Understanding Business Process Mapping

A **business process map** is essentially a flowchart that uses various symbols to illustrate each step in a business process. Business process mapping provides organizations with the ability to see how current business processes are actually completed. This can be useful to identify inefficiencies, bottlenecks, and variations on how different people complete the same process. Process mapping can also be used to see the differences in how the processes are actually completed versus how the processes were designed to be completed. Business process mapping is a big part of Six Sigma. **Six Sigma** is a set of techniques and tools developed by Motorola in 1986 to improve processes in a variety of industries.

Guidelines to Business Process Mapping

When developing a new system to replace an outdated process, taking the time to create a process map and obtaining feedback from the system's end users will ensure that the system is designed correctly. Below are a few guidelines to follow when creating a business process map.

Implementation Strategies—Gather information from the individuals who are involved in the business process about how it is completed. Be sure to inquire about whether or not the process changes if certain circumstances change. If the process being mapped is automated by a computer system, then the information is gathered by going through each step in the system.

Create a Process List—Creating a process list using the gathered information can be a good way to start the process mapping. A **process list** is simply a list of steps required to complete the process. It is typical to start by listing the first and last steps in the process, leaving plenty of room to list the steps in between. This can be done on paper, a whiteboard, a Word document using bulleted lists, or even an Excel spreadsheet. If the process being mapped involves various job positions and/ or departments, be sure to indicate those involved with each step. Similarly, if the process involves accessing multiple systems, be sure to indicate which systems are used in each step. Also, when creating the process list, be sure to consider any decision gates that must be dealt with in the process. A **decision gate** is a point in the process where a decision must be made. The next step in the process will be different based on the result of the decision.

When creating a process list, focus on the main actionable steps and avoid getting lost in the details of each step. When the process list is completed, verify its accuracy by running through the process yourself and/or having the users of the process sign off on it.

Business Process Mapping Symbols—There are common symbols used in business process mapping. Each symbol indicates a different kind of step. For those new to process mapping, it may be useful to include the symbols next to each of the steps in the process list.

An oval, or sometimes a rounded rectangle, is used to indicate the starting and ending points in the process.

A rectangle is used to indicate a step in the process.

Arrows are used to connect steps in a process and indicate the direction of the process flow.

A diamond is used to indicate a decision that must be made before the process can continue. For example, if a manager wants to be able to edit a timesheet in a payroll system, the decision may be "Are you a Manager?" If the answer is "Yes," then the process map should lead to a different step than if the answer is "No."

CONSIDER THIS | **How do you map a large process requiring multiple pages?**

When mapping more complex business processes, it is often necessary to utilize more than one page when printed. In this case, an additional symbol is used to indicate that the process continues on another page.

The figure below is an example of what a process list may look like.

Online Sales Process			
Role	**Step**	**System**	**Shape**
Customer	Sign-in to site	Web Browser	Start
Customer	Place items in cart	Web Browser	
Customer	Checks out	Web Browser	
System	Credit card authorization	Web Browser	
System	Authorization successful?	Web Browser	
System	No - Notify customer	Web Browser	
System	Yes - Continue with order	Web Browser	
System	Send order for fulfillment	Web Browser	
System	Provide confirmation number	Web Browser	End

Figure 1   Business process list example

Diagram the Process List—Once the process list has been created and reviewed for accuracy, it needs to be diagrammed. There are various business process mapping tools available, such as Microsoft Visio and SmartDraw. Simple process maps can also be created using the available shapes in Microsoft Word. Most business process maps start in the top-left corner and move from left to right and top to bottom.

Developing a Main User Interface for a Payroll System

When developing a user interface for any system, usability is one of the most important concepts to consider. Is the system easy and intuitive to use? Does it meet all the requirements of the managers and the employees? Does the design use colors that make the information easy to read? Should it incorporate any company colors, logos, etc.? Has it been thoroughly tested?

In order to ensure that users are able to log in based on their stored EmployeeIDs and passwords, as well as ensuring that only managers have access to the administration panel, you may find the DLookup function to be very useful. The **DLookup function** is used to retrieve the value of a particular field from a table that meets specified criteria. For example, it can be used to retrieve the stored password for an employee with a specific EmployeeID. That value can then be used as part of an IF statement to check to see if the password provided by the employee matches their stored password.

ACCESS CASE 5

QUICK REFERENCE	DLookup Function

Syntax: DLookup(expr, domain [,criteria])

- expr: Required. Identifies the field whose value you want to return, e.g., "[Password]".
- domain: Required. Identifies the table or query name where the value you want to return resides, e.g., "[tblEmployee]".
- criteria: Optional. The criteria to be used in order to select the desired value from the domain. Any field referenced in the criteria must also exist in the domain. The syntax required for criteria varies depending on whether the criterion is a text string, number, or a form field.

Here is an example of a DLookup function used to retrieve the last name of an employee that meets the criteria of the EmployeeID stored in a form field.

DLookup("[LastName]","[tblEmployee]","[EmployeeID] = '" & [frm_EmployeeID] & "'")

Note the use of concatenation to add single quotes around the field, since the field contains a text value.

Business Background

You have been provided with a partially created database that Bob's nephew had started before he realized that he was in a bit over his head. You will build on what he has started to create the main user interface for the Bob's Pizzeria payroll system. The tables included are as follows.

- tblAccount: Used to store data about each user account, including password and a password reset question and answer.
- tblClockIn-Out: Tracks the employee's clock-in and clock-out times.
- tblCurrentUser: Used to track the EmployeeID of the employee who is currently logged in.
- tblEmployee: Used to track employee information, such as name, address, and whether or not they are a manager.

Points of Concern

A fully functional system takes steps to prevent the most common user errors. With a payroll system, there are several potential user errors to consider, such as employees forgetting to clock in or out. As you build the system, consider how you will ensure that when an employee clocks out, the time is recorded with the most recent clock-in record and does not overwrite a previous entry.

Business Requirements

The managers at Bob's Pizzeria have taken the time to provide you with a business process map that will assist you in creating a finished user interface complete with the appropriate functionality to serve as their payroll system. You will need to create the necessary queries, forms, reports, and macros to make this system automated and user-friendly.

In addition to meeting the requirements laid out in the business process map, the payroll system main user interface must incorporate the following features:

- A login form that opens automatically when the database is opened using an AutoExec macro.
- Access is closed if the user cancels the login process.
- Option for an employee to view his or her time sheet report by providing a start date.
- The manager admin form should have access to edit any employee's time record as well as view a time sheet report for all employees by providing a start date.
- User's login data is deleted when the database is closed.
- Ensure users do not have direct access to the Navigation Pane.
- The system is visually appealing and consistently formatted across all forms.
- The system is user friendly and provides easy access to all the required features and tools.

MANAGER'S EMPHASIS
Usability
The manager wants to make sure the interface is simple and easy to use for all employees and managers.

Provided Files

Bob's Pizzeria Payroll Database ac05PayrollInterface.accdb	A partially created database. You will build on what is provided to create the main user interface for the payroll system.
Business Process Map for Payroll System ac05BusinessProcessMap.pdf	A process map illustrating the main processes that the payroll system interface must accommodate.

Analysis Questions

1. Explain how the design, functions, and features you incorporated into the system design enhanced usability.
2. How did the business process map help you build the system?
3. Explain the process you created to ensure that when an employee clocks out, the time is recorded with the most recent time record instead of overriding a previous time.
4. Describe the various macros that you created, both stand alone and embedded, and what purpose they serve in the system.
5. What other functionality do you think would be useful to incorporate into the system?

Deliverables

1. Submit the ac05PayrollInterface_LastFirst.accdb database and the ac05Login Data_LastFirst.txt file as directed by your instructor.
2. As directed by your instructor, submit the following.

   ac05Analysis_LastFirst.docx with your answers to the analysis questions.

   ac05Memo_LastFirst.docx to explain and document your solution.

ac05Presentation_LastFirst.pptx to present your recommendations, concerns, and findings to the analysis questions.

Post a video presentation to YouTube or other instructor-provided location with a duration of less than five minutes.

Checklist

- ☐ The solution allows for the business process to function as depicted in the process map.

- ☐ A login form opens automatically when the database is opened with the EmployeeID field empty.

- ☐ Access closes if the Cancel button is clicked on the login form.

- ☐ The solution accurately logs clock-in/clock-out times for each employee.

- ☐ An employee has the option to view a time sheet report and enter a start date for the report.

- ☐ A Manager Admin form is only visible to managers.

- ☐ A Manager Admin form has access to a time sheet report for all employees and prompts user for a start date for the report.

- ☐ Manager Admin form has access to edit time sheets for each employee.

- ☐ All forms are formatted consistently and are visually appealing.

- ☐ The solution is user-friendly and meets all requirements.

- ☐ A text file is provided that contains the login information for a manager and an employee.

- ☐ All analysis questions are answered thoroughly.

- ☐ The memo thoroughly explains and documents the solution.

- ☐ The PowerPoint presentation thoroughly presents recommendations, concerns, and findings to the analysis questions, including appropriate formatting.

- ☐ The YouTube video includes all required steps including appropriate formatting.

- ☐ All deliverables are completed and named correctly.

Key Terms

Business process map   30
Decision gate   30

DLookup function   32
Process list   30

Six Sigma   30

Implementing a New Information System

ADVANCED PROBLEM SOLVING CASES FOR MICROSOFT OFFICE 2016

REQUIRED SKILLS

1. Create select and action queries

2. Create reports

3. Create forms, subforms, and navigation forms

4. Create macros to automate and implement complex business logic

5. Create VBA procedures

6. Prepare a database for multiple users and modify the startup options

Business Dilemma

Developing an Inventory Management System for Sports Fanatics

Production & Operations

Frank Black is the owner of Sports Fanatics, a store that specializes in the acquisition and sale of authentic sports memorabilia. Sports Fanatics has been growing at a modest rate and has reached a point where Frank is in need of a more robust method of managing his inventory. You have been asked to develop an inventory management system using Microsoft Access. The system will include necessary tables, forms, reports, queries, and macros that will meet the requirements set forth by Frank.

MANAGER'S ADVICE ON THIS CASE

"Education and training are vital components to the success of any new system implementation. Without well-trained employees, even the most sophisticated systems can fail."

— Ja'Von Booker, small business owner

Files provided by the business:

- ac06InventoryData.csv
- ac06TeamsData.csv
- ac06RestockData.csv
- ac06SupplierData.csv
- ac06CustomerData.csv
- ac06RestockData2.csv

Deliverable files:

- ac06InventorySystem_LastFirst.accdb
- ac06InventorySystem_LastFirst_be.accdb
- ac06Analysis_LastFirst.docx
- ac06Memo_LastFirst.docx
- ac06Presentation_LastFirst.pptx
- ac06Video_LastFirst

Adopting an Implementation Strategy

Implementing a new system is a very challenging and time-consuming process for a business of any size. It is a common occurrence for the time needed for a full implementation of a new system to be grossly underestimated and undervalued. The time necessary for creating documentation, training users, and testing the system needs to be taken into consideration. One of the biggest factors that cause a system implementation to fail is inadequate training and education. To mitigate the risk of failure and to ensure that your employees are fully prepared for testing and training on the new system, it is recommended that companies create their own end-user documentation.

The Importance of Documentation

The purpose of end-user documentation is to provide the users of the system with all the information they need to fully understand the tasks so they can fully access all of the features of the system without the need for external resources. Creating quality end-user documentation requires intimate knowledge of the company's processes and procedures and nobody knows these things better than the employees. Therefore, end-user documentation should always be created by the end users themselves even if the company has hired an IT consulting firm to build and implement the new system. An added benefit of the end users creating the documentation is that it helps to further engrain the new processes and procedures into their memories and allows them to become involved and have some ownership in the overall implementation.

Developing end-user documentation for a new system can be quite daunting especially for complex systems that span multiple business functions. As with any large project, it can be better managed by breaking the project down into smaller tasks. It is important to note that end-user documentation is always a work in progress and it will continue to grow and change as system implementation begins and after the system is in production.

1. *Identify end users:* The first step to developing end-user documentation is to identify who the end users are. Decide which representatives from which departments will be developing the documentation. Be sure that each department or business function the new system impacts is represented in the group of end users.

2. *Choose a medium and create a template:* There are a variety of media options for end-user documentation, such as a printed manual, website, and wiki, to name a few. There are pros and cons to each medium. The important thing is to select whichever medium best fits the organization's needs. Creating a template for the overall document will create a consistent experience throughout the documentation, making it easy to navigate.

3. *Incorporate new work flows and procedures:* Whether the new system is replacing a manual process or a legacy system, there will most likely be changes in business processes. The new work flows and procedures need to be incorporated into the documentation. A **work flow** is a series of related topics, listed in chronological order, as they occur throughout the business processes. For example, consider the following:

   1. Prepare quotation

   2. Verify availability of goods

   3. Check customer credit

   4. Approve any special terms

   5. Process order

Each of these processes would be broken down and include precise instructions for completing the activity using the new system. Screen captures of the software should be used where appropriate so that the user can visually confirm he or she is performing the activity correctly.

4. *Testing:* The completion of the first draft of the end-user documentation should coincide with the testing phase of the system. The documentation can then be provided to those assigned to test the system and the documentation can be revised if necessary. It is also best practice to include a section outlining common problems or frequently asked questions.

5. *Final review and posting:* It is important to review the document after revisions have been incorporated to ensure that there are no obvious mistakes. Ensure that users are aware of how to access the documentation and encourage open communication of errors or instructions that are not clear so that the documentation can be improved.

6. *Maintenance:* Processes and procedures will change as the organization grows and evolves. It is essential that the documentation be continually updated and/or changed as needed.

Implementation Strategies

In order to increase the chance of a successful implementation, an appropriate implementation strategy should be adopted by the organization. There are several implementation strategies that have been proven successful. The four basic implementation strategies are as follows:

Direct Implementation—an implementation strategy that involves switching from the old system to the new system at the same time. With this strategy, the switchover date is typically scheduled ahead of time and often during a break in production or over a holiday period so that there is time to install the necessary hardware and software with minimal disruption.

Advantages

- Most rapid of all implementation strategies
- Minimizes risk of confusion between old and new systems

Disadvantages

- Most at risk of failure
- Most stressful for users as the previous system is not available if difficulty arises
- Most difficult to train staff as the new system was not available for training prior to implementation

Phased Implementation—an implementation strategy that involves introducing the new system in phases. After each phase is successfully completed, the next phase begins, eventually replacing the old system entirely.

Advantages

- Less risky, as it is a well-planned and controlled introduction and each phase is evaluated before continuing
- Training staff is easier as they are able to learn the skills required for each phase before moving on.

Disadvantages

- More time consuming than direct implementation
- Assessment of the entire system is delayed, since it comes only after all phases are introduced.

Pilot Implementation—an implementation strategy that involves replacing the old system with the new one at the same time but only for a selected subset of the user population. The pilot implementation could be for only one department in an organization or in one location. Once the pilot is considered a success, the pilot is extended until the old system is replaced entirely.

Advantages

- Lowest risk because if the pilot fails then not much is lost
- Easy to control because the pilot can be stopped if necessary
- Easy to evaluate success since both systems are still in operation

Disadvantages

- A slow process to move from pilot to full implementation
- System issues may not present themselves in small-scale pilots that occur with full implementation

Parallel Implementation—an implementation strategy where both old and new systems are used alongside each other. If the new system is a success, then the old system is stopped, and the new system is used exclusively.

Advantages

- Old system can still be used if new system presents issues
- Easy to evaluate because both systems are in use
- Easy to train staff by learning the new system while the old system is still operable

Disadvantages

- Not cost effective as both systems are fully operational and being supported
- Some risks associated with staff using two different systems for the same tasks

---

 CONSIDER THIS | **How do you select an appropriate implementation strategy?**

Careful consideration must be taken to ensure that the right strategy is adopted that best fits the scope of the system implementation and the culture of the organization.

Implementing a New Inventory Management System

Adopting and adhering to an implementation strategy is one important component in mitigating the risk of a new system failing. Of course, if the system being developed does not meet the business requirements, then regardless of how well the system is implemented, it will still be a failure.

Business Background

Frank Black is currently tracking orders and inventory himself, using an Excel workbook. He is manually recording each order and subtracting the number of units ordered from the number of units in stock after each order is requested. He has provided you with the worksheets from the workbook, saved as CSV files. You have been asked to develop an inventory management system using Microsoft Access and to recommend an implementation strategy to mitigate the risk of failure.

Frank has provided you with several text files including his inventory data, along with some sample data from his list of customers and suppliers, as well as a list of all the sports teams for which he buys and sells memorabilia.

Business Requirements

In order to build an effective database to help Frank manage his inventory, the data provided will need to be normalized into appropriate tables in order to reduce redundancy. Frank is not at all familiar with Microsoft Access so it is important that the system you develop be as user-friendly and as intuitive as possible.

Frank needs the system to meet the following requirements:

- Normalized tables with appropriate primary keys, data types, field sizes, lookup fields, formatting, input masks, etc.
- A new table to track orders placed with at least five sample orders entered.
- Before an order is placed, have the table check to make sure there is enough in inventory. If there is not, have a message display informing the user that there is not enough in inventory to place the order.
- Forms for entering new customers, suppliers, sports teams, orders, as well as any new categories of memorabilia he may acquire in the future.
- A form for entering items in inventory—must include a lookup function to search for a record with an ItemCode combo box.
- Form control buttons on each of the forms to navigate to other records, create new records, and delete records.
- A method using VBA and/or macros to import file(s) and automatically update the number of units in stock when one or multiple restock data files are imported.
- Be sure to incorporate error handling into your solution.
- Assign the procedure to a button on the inventory form.
- An inventory report where Frank can get a list of items that are at or under a specified number.
- A customer report showing all the orders placed for each customer.
- The database should be prepared in such a way that multiple users can place orders without conflicts.
- A Navigation Form from which all database objects can be accessed.
- Ensure that the appropriate startup preferences are set so that neither Frank nor his employees can inadvertently change objects.

MANAGER'S EMPHASIS
Good Database Design
Design is critical to ensure a system is easy to use and understand. Take the necessary steps to ensure ease of use.

Provided Files

Sports Fanatics Inventory ac06InventoryData.csv	A text file containing Sports Fanatics' current inventory of items.
Sports Teams ac06TeamsData.csv	A text file containing all the teams for which Sports Fanatics acquires and sells memorabilia.
Suppliers ac06SupplierData.csv	A text file containing a few individuals who routinely provide memorabilia for Sports Fanatics to sell.
Customers ac06CustomerData.csv	A text file containing a small sample set of customers.
Additional Inventory ac06RestockData.csv	A text file containing data regarding additional inventory of existing items.
Additional Inventory ac06RestockData2.csv	A text file containing data regarding additional inventory of existing items.

Analysis Questions

1. Which implementation strategy do you recommend Sports Fanatics adopt and why?
2. Explain how you ensured that an order cannot be placed if there are not enough items in inventory.
3. Explain the method you implemented for importing multiple restock files and updating the inventory items.
4. How did you make the system easy to use for those not familiar with Microsoft Access?

Deliverables

1. Submit the ac06InventorySystem_LastFirst.accdb database as directed by your instructor.
2. As directed by your instructor, submit the following.

   ac06Analysis_LastFirst.docx with your answers to the analysis questions.

   ac06Memo_LastFirst.docx to explain and document your solution.

   ac06Presentation_LastFirst.pptx to present your recommendations, concerns, and findings to the analysis questions.

   Post a video presentation to YouTube or other instructor-provided location with a duration of less than five minutes.

Checklist

☐ Normalized tables are created with appropriate field properties set.

☐ Forms are created for viewing, editing, and adding new records.

☐ Forms have navigation buttons added.

☐ Any unnecessary objects, such as the Navigation Pane and full Ribbon, are hidden.

☐ Inventory form includes a combo box of item codes used to look up an item's record.

☐ Before an order is placed, the database checks to make sure there is enough of the item in inventory.

☐ An inventory report is created that prompts for an inventory amount and displays all items that are less than or equal to the amount provided.

☐ A customer report is created showing all customers and their orders.

☐ A procedure is created that allows for multiple delimited files containing restocking data and automatically updates the inventory counts.

☐ Error handling is included in the import procedure.

☐ A Navigation Form is created with all objects logically grouped for easy access.

☐ Setup preferences are modified to prevent access to objects that could allow unintended changes.

☐ Database is split to enable multiple users to access the database.

☐ All analysis questions are answered thoroughly.

☐ The memo thoroughly explains and documents the solution.

☐ The PowerPoint presentation thoroughly presented recommendations, concerns, and findings to the analysis questions, including appropriate formatting.

☐ The YouTube video includes all required steps including appropriate formatting.

☐ All deliverables are completed and named correctly.

Key Terms

Creating Spreadsheet Models to Support Decisions

Excel Case 1 | ## ADVANCED PROBLEM SOLVING CASES FOR MICROSOFT OFFICE 2016

REQUIRED SKILLS

1. Create information with formulas and functions
2. Create named ranges
3. Use cell formatting to highlight important variables
4. Use financial, lookup, and IF functions
5. Visualize data with charts
6. Conduct what-if analysis

Business Dilemma

Terra Cotta Brew's Spreadsheet Model to Support Financial Decisions

Research & Development

The owners of Terra Cotta Brew Coffee Shop are looking to renovate and expand their coffee shop to create a more usable and relaxing space for their customers. They have already chosen a construction company to do the work and have received a quote for the cost of labor and materials. The estimated construction time is three months. The coffee shop will need to close completely for five days while the renovation work is completed. You have been asked to create a spreadsheet model to help the owners decide whether or not they can afford the proposed upgrades. You will model the situation using figures and estimates provided. You will conduct several different what-if analyses to determine which scenarios allow for the costs of the renovations to be paid in full in no more than seven years.

MANAGER'S ADVICE ON THIS CASE

"Spreadsheet models are extremely valuable with decision making. When designed well, they allow for easy what-if analysis and can provide decision makers with the information they need to make informed decisions."

—Esther Johnson, Financial Advisor

File provided by the business:

 ex01SalesData.xlsx

Deliverable files:

 ex01SpreadsheetModel_LastFirst.xlsx

ex01Analysis_LastFirst.docx

ex01Memo_LastFirst.docx

 ex01Presentation_LastFirst.pptx

ex01Video_LastFirst

Understanding Spreadsheet Models

There are two basic types of spreadsheet models: descriptive models and prescriptive or normative models. **Descriptive models** are used to describe the current state of a real-life situation. **Prescriptive models** attempt to suggest what should be done based on assumptions or standards and are extremely useful in decision making because they attempt to accurately predict future outcomes.

Two very common types of analysis used with spreadsheet models are scenario analysis and sensitivity analysis. **Scenario analysis** is conducted by changing certain variables to meet a given set of conditions or scenarios. It is commonly used to see the outcome of the most-likely scenario, worst-case scenario, and best-case scenario. **Sensitivity analysis** is conducted by observing the changes to an output of a model, such as profit, by changing one or more of the variables, such as demand. Sensitivity analysis helps to determine which variables have the biggest impact on the output.

The Basic Components of Spreadsheet Models

Although descriptive and prescriptive spreadsheet models have different purposes in business, they do share common components. A spreadsheet model relies on inputs. **Inputs** are known facts about a person, place, thing, or event that affect a situation. For example, inputs may include the number of items sold and the cost of raw materials. Spreadsheet models also include decision variables and uncertain variables. **Decision variables** are controllable inputs that a decision maker can change, usually within defined constraints, for the current situation. An example of a decision variable might be determining the quantity of raw materials to order. **Uncertain variables** are uncontrollable inputs that affect the situation but are not controlled directly by a decision maker. An example of an uncertain variable might be the demand for a particular product. Spreadsheet models also include outputs. **Outputs** are values of interest that are the result of calculations involving inputs, decision variables, and uncertain variables. Spreadsheet models typically have several different outputs, but typically only one or two are considered primary. The figure below shows a diagram of the basic components that make up a spreadsheet model.

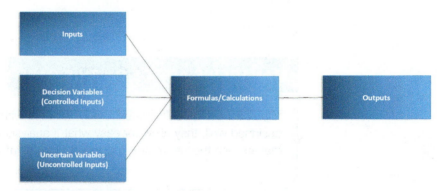

Figure 1 Basic components of a spreadsheet model

QUICK REFERENCE	Basic Spreadsheet Model Components

- Inputs: Known facts about a person, place, thing, or event that affect a situation.
- Decision Variables: Controllable inputs that a decision maker can change.
- Uncertain Variables: Uncontrollable inputs that affect the situation but are not controlled directly by a decision maker.
- Outputs: Values of interest that are the result of calculations involving inputs, decision variables, and uncertain variables.

The Basic Design Principles of Spreadsheet Models

Since spreadsheet models are used in decision making, they must be easy to use and understand and easily adapt to changing variables. There are five basic design principles that you should take into consideration when creating spreadsheet models:

- **Accuracy**—The most important design principle. You must carefully verify the accuracy of your inputs and ensure that your model's outputs are correct. If a model is not accurate, then decisions based on the model will be poor.

- **Clarity**—A spreadsheet model should effectively communicate its content to other people or users. Formatting values appropriately and consistently as well as using specific text labels, including units of measure, increase clarity.

- **Flexibility**—Spreadsheet models need to easily adapt to changing variables. Use cell references instead of entering values directly into formulas and functions.

- **Efficiency**—The more complex a spreadsheet model becomes, the longer it may take to update with changes. Taking advantage of the many available functions instead of creating complex mathematical formulas will create a more efficient model.

- **Documentation**—Further explains the purpose of the spreadsheet model and provides any additional information about the model to other people. There are two types of documentation:

    - **External**—Typically in the form of a Word document, includes general information about the model, such as the author, purpose, software used, etc.

    - **Internal**—Descriptive row and column headings, a list of named ranges used, inputs and outputs organized logically, in-cell comments, etc.

 CONSIDER THIS | **Are All of the Design Principles Important?**

As mentioned above, accuracy is the most important design principle, but all the other principles are also very important. What problems could arise if any one of the other design principles was not taken into consideration?

Creating Spreadsheet Models to Support Decisions

The goal of most spreadsheet models is to make them as simple as possible by incorporating only enough details to meet the requirements and omitting any unnecessary or irrelevant details. The first steps for creating a spreadsheet model are the same as for any other development project: planning and requirements gathering.

It is recommended to take some time to sketch out an overall plan before starting Excel.

- The inputs need to be identified as well as any decision variables, uncertain variables, and the primary outputs of interest.

- Inputs, decision variables, and uncertain variables should be grouped together logically. Color-coded schemes are typically used so that users can easily identify the different variables of interest.

- Determine the key inputs, decision variables, uncertain variables, and outputs to highlight in the model. Highlighting these key variables will make conducting what-if analysis with the model much easier.

- Determine the formulas and functions necessary to relate the inputs and variables to the outputs. If the calculations are complicated, it is a good idea to break them down into simpler formulas so that any errors can be easily identified and corrected.

Taking the time to plan ahead will result in much less time and frustration when troubleshooting and debugging a completed model.

Business Background

The owners of the Terra Cotta Brew Coffee Shop have provided you with some details about the finances of the business and the estimated cost of the renovation and expansion below.

- Previous year sales revenue: Provided by business in ex01SalesData.xlsx
- Previous year costs: 80% of revenue
- Amount available for investment: $90,000–$150,000
- Estimated cost of renovations, including two scenarios: $450,000 to complete the project in three months, or $475,000 to complete the project a few weeks early
- Estimated profit growth rate post renovation:
  - Year 1: 9.25%
  - Year 2: 10%
  - Year 3: 8.25%
  - Years 4–7: 5.0%
- APR for a bank loan ranging from 5.0% to 7.3% for a 5-year short-term loan. The APR is dependent on how much needs to be financed—the more needed, the lower the interest rate.

Amount to Finance	APR
$300,000.00	7.3%
$310,000.00	7.0%
$320,000.00	6.5%
$330,000.00	6.0%
$340,000.00	5.5%
$360,000.00	5.0%

Points of Concern

If a spreadsheet model is not easy to understand, then others may misinterpret the data, which may also lead to poor decisions. When developing spreadsheet models, each of the design principles must be taken into consideration, and it must be flexible enough to easily accommodate what-if analysis.

Business Requirements

MANAGER'S EMPHASIS
Ease of Use
The spreadsheet model needs to be easy to use and interpret by several decision makers with a variety of experience with Excel.

The owners of the Terra Cotta Brew Coffee Shop need your help with some decisions about the renovation. They need a well-designed spreadsheet model that will incorporate all the necessary inputs, decision variables, uncertain variables, and outputs to determine how much to invest, how much to borrow, and whether or not to pay extra to expedite the renovation. The decision will be based on the estimated growth rates in profits after the renovation is complete and whether or not those additional profits will be enough to pay off the amount borrowed in seven years or less. All profit amounts above the last year's profits will go toward paying off the loan. The spreadsheet model must include the following:

- Calculations for last year's revenue, costs, and profit; amount needed to finance; and total cost of the loan, including interest payments, for monthly and quarterly payment options.

- Estimated profit earnings for each of the next seven years.
- Estimated profit earnings over last year's profit earnings for each of the next seven years.
- Total estimated additional profit earnings at the end of seven years.
- Key inputs, decision variables, and uncertain variables, as well as key outputs identified with in-cell comments and highlighting.
- Appropriate formatting, text labels, named ranges, and organization throughout the model.
- A line chart to show estimated profits post renovation for the next seven years compared to current profits remaining the same without the renovations.

Provided File

Terra Cotta Brew's sales data	File contains data on units sold from 2016.
ex01SalesData.xlsx	

Analysis Questions

1. What is the purpose of a spreadsheet model and how can a spreadsheet model help the owners of the Terra Cotta Brew Coffee Shop make decisions about the renovation?
2. Which variables did you indicate as your key inputs, decision variables, uncertain variables, and outputs? Why?
3. Describe how you incorporated each of the design principles into your spreadsheet model.
4. Assuming that the investment amount is $137,000 and the estimated growth rates are accurate, should the owners go with a monthly or quarterly payment plan? Why?
5. Which kinds of what-if analysis should be conducted to ensure a good decision is made?
6. Explain a scenario where you would not recommend the owners invest in the renovations.

Deliverables

1. Submit the ex01SpreadsheetModel_LastFirst.xlsx workbook as directed by your instructor.
2. As directed by your instructor, submit the following.

    ex01Analysis_LastFirst.docx with your answers to the analysis questions.

    ex01Memo_LastFirst.docx to explain and document your solution.

    ex01Presentation_LastFirst.pptx to present your recommendations, concerns, and findings to the analysis questions.

    Post a video presentation to YouTube or other instructor-provided location with a duration of less than five minutes.

Checklist

☐ Revenue, Costs, and Profits are calculated with appropriate formatting.

☐ IF statement is used to determine renovation costs.

☐ Amount needed to finance is calculated with appropriate formatting.

☐ APR of loan is determined with a LOOKUP function.

☐ Total cost of loan is calculated for both monthly and quarterly payments.

☐ Primary input variables are identified with formatting and comments.

☐ Uncertain variables are identified with formatting and comments.

☐ Primary output variables are identified with formatting and comments.

☐ Estimated annual profit earnings are calculated each year for the next seven years.

☐ Total additional profits earned is calculated.

☐ Line chart is created to compare estimated profit growth to stagnant growth for the next seven years.

☐ Appropriate named ranges are used throughout the model to add clarity.

☐ Values are labeled clearly and organized logically.

☐ All deliverables are completed and named correctly.

Key Terms

Accuracy 47	Documentation, External 47	Outputs 46
Clarity 47	Documentation, Internal 47	Prescriptive models 46
Decision variables 46	Efficiency 47	Scenario analysis 46
Descriptive models 46	Flexibility 47	Sensitivity analysis 46
Documentation 47	Inputs 46	Uncertain variables 46

Evaluating a Plan of Action with a Decision Support System

Excel Case 2 | ## ADVANCED PROBLEM SOLVING CASES FOR MICROSOFT OFFICE 2016

REQUIRED SKILLS

1. Build nested IF functions
2. Work with data and information in data tables
3. Integrate conjunction functions into IF functions
4. Create a LOOKUP function
5. Use the SUBTOTAL function and filters in a data table
6. Develop and customize a PivotTable and PivotChart
7. Create conditional statistical and math functions

Business Dilemma

Evaluating Whether Business Policies Are Being Followed

Research & Development

Tropical Travel Agency has hired a consulting firm to audit some of its existing business processes to ensure that the business is running efficiently and effectively. You have been asked to analyze existing data and create a spreadsheet that will be used to ensure group fees are being applied to clients correctly. Additionally, you will create a form that will make it easier for all travel agents to take reservations and determine which fees should be assessed based on whether the client is booking a reservation for a group, family, or individual.

MANAGER'S ADVICE ON THIS CASE

"Different levels of management make different types of decisions. As an information technology professional, understanding what each level's information needs are so they can make sound decisions is critical because you most likely will be providing that information to each manager. Managers use decision support systems to help with the decision making process and their decisions are only as good as the information they obtain from existing systems within the organization."

—Jack Hanson, Chief Information Officer

Files provided by the business:

 ex02TravelAgency.xlsx

ex02TransactionData.txt

Deliverable files:

 ex02TravelAgency_LastFirst.xlsx

 ex02Analysis_LastFirst.docx

ex02Memo_LastFirst.docx

 ex02Presentation_LastFirst.pptx

 ex02Video_LastFirst

Understanding Decision Support Systems

A **decision support system** (DSS) is any system that helps support the decision-making process and assists the management and strategic levels of an organization. DSSs help make unstructured and semi-structured decisions, which may be constantly changing and not easily identified in advance. Even an Excel spreadsheet can serve as a DSS. An important note is that a DSS should support management's decision making, not replace the manager.

Decision making has been described as a process that includes three phases—intelligence, design, and choice. In the **intelligence phase**, the decision maker asks, "Is there a problem?" Information is collected that will help identify the problems that have been occurring. This information can be from inside or outside of the organization and can include information on possible ways to solve the problem. In the **design phase**, the decision maker asks, "What are the alternatives?" Possible solutions to the problem are considered along with choosing the model to process the data. Finally, in the **choice phase**, the decision maker asks, "Which alternative do I choose?" and one of the various solution alternatives is selected.

QUICK REFERENCE	Components of a Decision Support System

- Data management module: Consists of current or historical data and possibly some external data. Included are the capabilities to manipulate the data. Historical data may be retrieved from a data warehouse.
- Model management module: Contains a collection of mathematical models such as statistical models, linear programming, forecasting, and sensitivity analysis models that are available for the user. This may also include OLAP or data mining tools.
- Dialog management module: Includes the interface between the users and other modules. Additionally, this module displays the analysis of results.

Decision Making in Business

Different levels of management have different decisions that need to be made. Some managers simply rely on their gut when making decisions. However, when managers combine reasoning and data along with technology, they make better choices and their organizations benefit as well.

The management pyramid is a model that separates managers into three levels including operational management, tactical or middle management, and strategic management. The pyramid shape illustrates the quantity of managers at each level within the organization.

Figure 1 Management Pyramid

Strategic management describes executives such as C-level managers—CEO, CFO, CIO, COO, and so forth—and other senior managers within an organization. The actual title of a manager does not distinguish whether a manager is a strategic manager. It depends upon the organization. For example, many organizations have a reasonable number of managers who have the title of vice president, such as vice president of finance and vice president of human resources. However, the banking and investment industries are very different than the norm. In large brokerage firms and investment banks, there are usually several vice presidents in each local branch office, and at best, they are tactical managers. The title is sometimes more of a marketing approach for customers than denoting an actual managerial position within the company because customers feel more confident speaking with someone with whom they believe to be in control and knowledgeable about the business.

The decisions that strategic managers make are unstructured. An **unstructured decision** is one that does not have an optimal solution. For example, strategic managers of a retailer determine if the company should open new stores over the next so many years. They first need to determine what organizational goals would be achieved by doing so. One may think that finding a location for the new store is the main task; however, it is only a small part of the process. Strategic managers have to determine if they will build a new building or renovate an existing building, evaluate demographics to ensure that the organization's revenue goals will be met based on population and target market, evaluate surrounding competition, and determine ease of access for both customers and suppliers. These are just a few of the items these managers evaluate prior to opening a new storefront. These nonroutine decisions require the decision maker to provide judgment, evaluation, and insight because there is no agreed-upon method for making the decision.

Tactical management is also known as middle management, meaning these managers have not reached the C-level status, but they are not entry-level managers either. Think about the last time you went to the mall. Many of the stores you went into or walked by have regional managers, district managers, or both, depending on the size of the retailer. These positions qualify as tactical managers because they are more hands-on than the strategic managers but not nearly as hands-on as the operational managers.

The decisions that tactical managers make are **semi-structured decisions**. The decisions contain both unstructured and structured components, where only part of the problem has a clear-cut answer determined by a suitable process—it contains both subjective and objective elements. For example, after analyzing the competition, demographics, and target market in Pittsburgh, PA, the CEO decided that the organization should consider opening three new stores based on his findings. He enlists his regional manager to find five possible locations from which the CEO can choose. The regional manager can use mathematic equations to determine the distance from existing company stores and competitors, but would need to use judgment, evaluation, and insight in order to determine whether a location would provide a good option to the retailer based on criteria such as ease of access.

Operational management, the first-line managers or supervisors who work in every unit in an organization, are responsible for the daily management of the line workers. Although first-level managers generally do not set goals for the organization, they have a very strong influence on the company because these are the managers that most employees interact with on a daily basis.

The decisions that operational managers make are structured decisions. **Structured decisions** are those that only have one optimal solution. For example, $2 + 2 = 4$ because the problem has processes in place that help one solve it. These decisions have an organized approach to developing and evaluating innovative options and making justifiable choices.

 CONSIDER THIS | **Why Use a Pyramid?**

Nearly every business publication focused on management uses a pyramid to diagram the different levels of management. Why do you think the shape is significant?

Evaluating a Plan of Action with a Decision Support System

When using an Excel workbook throughout your organization, it is a good idea to ensure that data is being entered correctly. You would not want employees either accidentally or purposely giving items away at no charge. For example, groups that book a trip receive a group discount. The manager would not want individuals receiving the same discount.

Business Background

Tropical Travel Agency wants you to audit some of its existing business processes to ensure that the business is running efficiently and effectively. The manager has provided you with some details about the business below. The worksheets included in the workbook are as follows.

- Agency Clients: Used to track all customers who have booked at least one time through the agency.
- Travel Packages: Used to track all travel packages offered at the agency and the agent responsible for managing the travel package.

- Client Transactions: Will be used to track the travel packages purchased by clients.
- Agency Data and Analysis: Used to track the agency's internal data such as commissions, discount rates, transaction rankings, and named ranges.

Additional details include the following.

- Sample transaction data: Provided by business in ex02TransactionData.txt.
- Commission rates are as follows:

Years Employed	Commission Rate
5 Years or less	5.0%
Between 6 and 10 years	7.0%
11 or more years	10.0%

- Commissions are calculated on the travel packages and adjusted by payroll when the trips are booked.
- Reward Points for agency's loyalty program.

Points Earned	Discount %
200	2.5%
400	5.0%
600	7.5%
800	10.0%
1000	15.0%

Points of Concern

Although a workbook has been created for you, the workbook's design needs to be modified so that it is easier to use and has more functionality. For example, you will need to insert a nested IF function that will determine the discount a customer will receive. Think about how this will change the workbook's functionality and interface.

Business Requirements

The manager, Joe Madison, has been using an Excel workbook to store information about the agency. Currently, he saves all client transactions in a separate text file. He would like all of the data to be available in one workbook, making it easier to manage his business. For instance, it would be helpful to have information readily available so that Mr. Madison can prepare a budget for agent commissions, estimate profit earnings over the next year, manage the agency's customer loyalty program, and manage the vacation packages by popularity and ranking.

Mr. Madison also believes it would be a good idea to analyze some of the data he has collected. This will help determine which trips are the most popular and how many rewards program points his customers have earned, just to name a few. The spreadsheet model must include the following.

- Clients named range formatted as a table and matches the color scheme of the entire workbook. Create named ranges for all columns within the table. Insert a formula that looks up the Reward Points Year-to-Date (YTD) based on the Total Spent.
- Based on all of the data in the table, use formulas or functions to calculate the maximum and average amounts that all clients spent.
- Create an advanced filter that finds all customers who have spent more than $6,000.

MANAGER'S EMPHASIS
Facilitating Decision Making
Consider how the data will be used and what formulas and functions can help manipulate the data.

- Use a formula or function to calculate the Total Customers and Total Spent based on the rows that are displaying in the table.
- The ex02TransactionData.txt data should be imported to the labeled location within the workbook. Using the imported data along with data in the workbook, calculate the Cost of Trip, Discount, and Total After Discount.
- Commission pay for imported data.
- Number of transactions and totals for transaction rankings.
- Advanced filter of Charlie's clients who spent more than $5,000 with the results pasted below.
- A PivotTable and PivotChart that analyzes the revenue generated after discounts for each Florida travel package by date booked and client's last name. Florida travel packages include Ft. Lauderdale, Orlando, and St. Lucia.
- Appropriate formatting, text labels, named ranges, and organization throughout the spreadsheet model.

Provided Files

Travel agency workbook ex02TravelAgency.xlsx	A snapshot of the travel agency data.
Transactions text file ex02TransactionData.txt	A text file that currently houses recent client transactions.

Analysis Questions

1. How will the spreadsheet model help Mr. Madison monitor key information? How would his business benefit from being able to retrieve key information on a regular basis?
2. List three decisions that Mr. Madison can make using the data in the workbook and what type of decision each is—structured, unstructured, or semi-structured.
3. Describe how you incorporated appropriate formatting, text labels, named ranges, and organization throughout the spreadsheet model.
4. How did the management pyramid influence your decisions?
5. What is the purpose of offering discounts? Do you think that clients are saving too much money, possibly causing negative consequences for the agency?
6. Do you have any recommendations for future changes to the spreadsheet model that would better suit the agency?

Deliverables

1. Submit the ex02TravelAgency_LastFirst.xlsx workbook as directed by your instructor.
2. As directed by your instructor, submit the following.

   ex02Analysis_LastFirst.docx with your answers to the analysis questions.

   ex02Memo_LastFirst.docx to explain and document your solution.

   ex02Presentation_LastFirst.pptx to present your recommendations, concerns, and findings to the analysis questions.

   Post a video presentation to YouTube or other instructor-provided location with a duration of less than five minutes.

Checklist

- ☐ Named ranges are created and used throughout the spreadsheet model.

- ☐ All functions are created and include appropriate formatting.

- ☐ Advanced filters are created.

- ☐ Data is imported into the spreadsheet model.

- ☐ All formulas are created and include appropriate formatting.

- ☐ A PivotTable and PivotChart are created, customized, and include appropriate formatting.

- ☐ Appropriate formatting, text labels, named ranges, and organization are used throughout the spreadsheet model.

- ☐ All analysis questions are answered thoroughly.

- ☐ The memo thoroughly explains and documents the solution.

- ☐ The PowerPoint presentation thoroughly presents recommendations, concerns, and findings to the analysis questions, including appropriate formatting.

- ☐ The YouTube video includes all required steps, including appropriate formatting.

- ☐ All deliverables are completed and named correctly.

Key Terms

Choice phase   52
Decision support system   52
Design phase   52
Intelligence phase   52

Operational
   management   54
Semi-structured
   decision   54

Strategic management   53
Structured decision   54
Tactical management   53
Unstructured decision   53

Excel Simulation with Sensitivity and Risk Analysis

Excel Case 3 | ## ADVANCED PROBLEM SOLVING CASES FOR MICROSOFT OFFICE 2016

REQUIRED SKILLS

1. Use VLOOKUP and INDEX functions
2. Build nested IF functions
3. Work with data and information in data tables
4. Use statistical functions such as AVERAGE, MIN, MAX, STDEV.S, and QUARTILE
5. Create conditional statistical functions using the AVERAGEIF function
6. Analyze output using a scatter chart and a box and whisker chart

Business Dilemma

Evaluating the Risk of Healthcare Plan Pricing

Research & Development

County Line Insurance Agency sells many different lines of insurance including homeowner, renters, automotive, healthcare, and life. Management is trying to create a better method of determining policy pricing. As an actuary who has been working for County Line Insurance Agency for nearly a decade, you have been asked to analyze existing health insurance data and create a predictive model that will be used to ensure customers are being charged the correct premium.

MANAGER'S ADVICE ON THIS CASE

"The main goal of sensitivity and risk analyses is to increase understanding of how the decision making inputs will affect your final choice. This method encompasses multiple techniques of changing input variables in the spreadsheet model to see the effect on the output."

—Joshua Mordake, Investment Manager

File provided by the business:

 ex03Healthcare.xlsx

Deliverable files:

 ex03Healthcare_LastFirst.xlsx    ex03Presentation_LastFirst.pptx

ex03Analysis_LastFirst.docx   ex03Video_LastFirst

 ex03Memo_LastFirst.docx

Understanding Simulation with Sensitivity and Risk Analysis

Simulation analysis is the process of modeling a situation under uncertainty to predict the statistical probability of potential outcomes. While simulation is a predictive model, it does not predict the future like a fortuneteller. A fortuneteller would tell a client she will have "3 children." Simulation would tell the same client that there is a 10% chance she will have 1 child, a 60% chance she will have 2 children, a 20% chance she will have 3 children, and continued on for all the possible number of children, including no children. In a simulation, the model is specific to the situation and not just societal averages. The probability that a 45-year-old childless woman will have 10 children is most likely nearing 0%. Simulation is very specific to an individual circumstance. Simulation analysis provides a model to account for uncertainty in a customized and individualistic way. If a model has many assumptions, simulation analysis is better than analyses such as optimization. Using optimization—such as the Solver add-in in Excel—works best when assumptions are minimal or inconsequential. While beyond the scope of this case, a model can be simulated and then optimized afterward in some situations.

Sensitivity analysis, related to what-if analysis, is used to evaluate the impact of a variable on the outcome of a model. If a change in the value of a variable causes significant change to the outcome, then the model is sensitive to that variable. For example, different companies are impacted by the price of gas. Any university is impacted by a change in gas price, relating to travel, supply shipping costs, and other miscellaneous ways. However, a trucking company is much more sensitive! Every mile driven increases overall costs and decreases profit. In this example, a trucking company is very sensitive to gas price whereas a university is minimally sensitive to gas price.

As an important component of the overall risk management strategy, an organization needs to perform a sensitivity analysis on its portfolio. Whether the organization is public or private, a manufacturer that obtains raw materials from both within the United States as well as overseas, a technology developer that offshores the development of smartphone apps, or a service-based organization that deals in foreign currencies, almost every organization will experience risk of some kind such as interest rate, foreign exchange, or commodity risk. Additionally, it is highly likely that an organization will face more than one of these risks. Because of this, management needs to be able to evaluate how these risks will impact their business.

Decision Making with Heuristics

One method of decision making involves heuristics. Heuristics play an important role in both problem solving and decision making. A **heuristic** is a mental shortcut that allows a person to solve problems and make judgments quickly and efficiently. When someone makes a decision based on deductive reasoning rather than by following a predetermined method or formula, the chosen solution is not guaranteed to be the optimal choice.

 **CONSIDER THIS** | **What Other Decisions Can Be Made Using Heuristics?**

Besides business, heuristics can be used in many industries such as law, psychology, and philosophy. When people are trying to solve a problem or make a decision, they often turn to heuristics when they need a quick solution. What kind of decisions can you make using this methodology?

Trial and error is one of the most common heuristics. For example, the drug industry has customarily used trial and error as the main method of finding new drugs, such as antibiotics. Babies use trial and error when learning to walk, and teenagers may use trial and error when learning how to drive a car. However, this methodology would not work for a member of the military or police who is learning how to diffuse a bomb.

QUICK REFERENCE	Examples of Heuristic Methods

- Trial and error—A way of finding the best solution by trying out one or more methods and then noting and eliminating errors.
- Rule of thumb—A method of assessment that is made according to a practical rule and not based on science or a precise measurement.
- Educated guess—A method of guessing which choice is the best based on experience or theoretical knowledge.
- Common sense—The ability to recognize, comprehend, and evaluate a problem where the decision can be realistically expected of nearly all people without any need for debate.

Controlling for Conditions of Uncertainty

Business decision making is almost always combined with uncertain conditions, and poor decisions can affect an organization's bottom line. Understandably, the more informed the decision maker is, the better the decision will be. Treating decisions as a gamble—a tradeoff of the value of a specific outcome against its probability—is the foundation of decision theory.

According to D. Warner North, **decision theory** is a theoretical structure for decision making that takes ambiguity into account. As a result, decision making becomes an optimization problem, and mathematical programming or data modeling may be used to obtain a solution. There is a difference between a good decision and a good outcome. For example, suppose that Company A is considering four investment alternatives: investing $1 million, investing $750,000, investing $500,000, or not investing at all. Company A has four options that are in its control; however, only one choice can be made. The consequences of the investment, in terms of profit or loss, are dependent on the market and beyond Company A's control.

RETURN ON INVESTMENT (PROFIT)

Investment	Strong Market	Fair Market	Poor Market
$1,000,000	$100,000	$25,000	–$50,000
$750,000	$75,000	$18,750	–$37,500
$500,000	$50,000	$12,500	–$25,000

Table 1 Company A's investment choices

Sensitivity analysis can be used to determine the risk factors when making a choice and then help develop priorities for risk mitigation. **Risk mitigation** consists of developing options that will enhance opportunities and reduce threats of the choice being made. **Risk assessment** offers structured information that allows decision makers to pinpoint interventions that can lead to improving a situation or to avoiding future problems. Thus, the objective of risk assessment is to answer three questions.

- What could go wrong?
- How likely is it to happen?
- What would be the consequences if it did?

Perhaps Manufacturer C wants to assess the level of risk it will be taking if it produces a specific quantity of rubber ducks. In other words, what will the effect be on net income? With a wholesale price of $3, Manufacturer C believes it will sell between 2,000 and 3,000 units. Additionally, Manufacturer C has to take into account fixed costs of $4,761 and a variable cost of $0.36 per unit. The company could perform a manual what-if analysis to determine its net income by creating a model in Excel and physically entering values in the Inputs section.

	A	B
1	**Inputs**	
2	Unit price	$ 3.00
3	Units sold	2,500
4	**Expenses**	
5	Unit variable cost	$ 0.36
6	Fixed cost	$ 4,761
7	**Net Income**	$ 1,839

Table 2   Spreadsheet model

	A	B
1	**Inputs**	
2	Unit price	$ 3.00
3	Units sold	2,500
4	**Expenses**	
5	Unit variable cost	$ 0.36
6	Fixed cost	$ 4,761
7	**Net Income**	=B3*(B2-B5)-B6

Table 3   Formula view

Additionally, Manufacturer C would most likely be interested in determining its **cost of lost profits**—when an organization suffers a loss of income due to an unforeseen circumstance. For example, assume the manufacturer has a backlog of rubber duck orders. During production, a machine is used that generates revenues of $1,000 per hour, but incurs incremental costs and expenses of $250, deriving $750 per hour of contribution margin. Unfortunately, poor maintenance of the machine resulted in the production line shutting down for 10 hours. The repair bill—repairs and maintenance costs—to fix the machine was $1,500. But, the company also lost $7,500—10 hours × $750 per hour—in operating or pre-tax income. Thus, the manufacturer experienced a cost of lost profits of $9,000.

Organizations are generally more interested in how the inputs will affect all available choices that could be selected. Excel offers what-if analysis tools, such as Solver, data tables, Scenario Manager, and Goal Seek, to help managers. However, what if management wants to perform predictive modeling based off of random numbers that Excel would select on its own? **Predictive modeling** is the method in which a model is created or chosen to attempt to best predict the probability of an outcome. The random numbers would be based on what management anticipates the numbers to be, and Excel would serve as a simulation.

Predictive modeling using simulation is needed to help people make decisions and plays a vital role in business. People can only process six to eight variables at a time, whereas the algorithms contained within a predictive model can analyze hundreds of variables to make a diagnosis or a prediction of risk. In the United States, many industries use predictive modeling as a way to control costs. For example, the healthcare industry uses predictive modeling to determine future healthcare costs based on prior costs, demographics, and diagnoses. From automotive to homeowner policies, the insurance industry uses predictive modeling to determine how much each customer should be charged. Even an e-mail client can use predictive modeling to determine the probability that an e-mail is spam.

Predictive modeling can be done with sophisticated software tools such as @Risk or Crystal Ball. These tools allow the modeler to specify the distribution for which software picks out the variable. For example, the modeler could say that demand is expected at a normal distribution with a mean of 10,000 and a standard deviation of 1,000. A modeler can determine the distribution based on past performance or experience. Excel is unable to do this by itself. However, simulating the results is still possible.

The =RAND() function in Excel will generate a random decimal between 0 and 1. The value will change every time the spreadsheet refreshes. Pressing the F9 key will force a refresh to get Excel to pick new numbers. However, most of the time, a variable is not evenly distributed, which is what the RAND function will produce. In other words, there is a 50% chance of getting a decimal under 0.5 and 50% chance of getting a decimal over 0.5. Excel can still use a distribution by using the RAND function with a cumulative probabilities table.

CONSIDER THIS | Can =RAND() Truly Be Random?

Any function in Excel is generated through a mathematical formula. If a mathematical formula generates the random number, can it really be random?

First, the modeler must determine the individual probabilities. Illustratively, suppose the model simulates weekly profit at four potential weekly demands. There is a 10% chance that the demand will be 1,000 units, a 35% chance that the demand will be 1,500 units, a 40% chance that the demand will be 2,000 units, and a 15% chance that the demand will be 2,500 units. Notice the percentages all add up to 100%. To create the cumulative probabilities, start with 0 and then add the decimal percentage for the outcome to create a table similar to the following.

	A	B
1	Individual Probabilities	Cumulative Probability
2	0.1	0
3	0.35	0.1
4	0.4	0.45
5	0.15	0.85

Table 4 Probability Table view

	A	B	C
1	Individual Probabilities	Cumulative Probability	Demand Outcome
2	0.1	0	1000
3	0.35	=B2+A2	1500
4	0.4	=B3+A3	2000
5	0.15	=B4+A4	2500

Table 5 Probability Table formula view

Then, the modeler can use a RAND function in a VLOOKUP across the array of Cumulative Probability and Demand Outcome columns to find the weighted outcome. The model is then completed once the outcome—or what needs to be evaluated—is calculated. Suppose the following simplistic model of profit is a function of demand.

	A	B
7	Ordered	2,000
8	Demand	2,000
9	Price	$ 10
10	Revenue	$ 20,000
11	Wholesale Price	$ 5
12	Fixed Costs	$ 5,000
13	Variable Costs	$ 10,000
14	Profit	$ 5,000

Table 6　Weighted Outcome view

	A	B
7	Ordered	2000
8	Demand	=VLOOKUP(RAND(),B2:C5,2,TRUE)
9	Price	10
10	Revenue	=B8*MIN(B7,B8)
11	Wholesale Price	5
12	Fixed Costs	5000
13	Variable Costs	=B7*B11
14	Profit	=B10-B12-B13

Table 7　Weighted Outcome formula view

After the model of a single instance is created, then the simulation consists of many iterations of that one instance. This can be accomplished using a one-way data table in Excel. The first column is the iteration number, and the second column is the outcome—here, profit. The data table's column input cell should reference a completely blank cell. This will cause Excel to put the iteration number into that blank cell and force the model to refresh. In essence, it is nearly identical to pressing the F9 key to draw a new random number and, thus, weighted outcome. Below is an example of a 100 iteration data table simulation—note that rows 20 through 114 are hidden and that cell G12 is a blank cell.

	A	B
16	Simulation	
17	Iteration	$ 5,000
18	1	$ 5,000
19	2	$ 10,000
115	98	$ (5,000)
116	99	$ 10,000
117	100	$ –

Table 8　Simulation view

	A	B
16	Simulation	
17	Iteration	=B14
18	1	=TABLE(,G12)
19	2	=TABLE(,G12)
115	98	=TABLE(,G12)
116	99	=TABLE(,G12)
117	100	=TABLE(,G12)

Table 9　Simulation formula view

Lastly, the modeler will then calculate statistics based on the iterations of calculations in the model. At a minimum, the statistics should include the average, minimum, maximum, and standard deviation. Routinely, other statistics such as quartiles are also calculated. Below is an example from this scenario.

	A	B
119	Stats	
120	Average	$ 2,550
121	Max	$ 10,000
122	Min	$ (5,000)
123	Standard Deviation	$ 4,394
124	# below 0	14

Table 10　Statistics view

	A	B
119	Stats	
120	Average	=AVERAGE(B18:B117)
121	Max	=MAX(B18:B117)
122	Min	=MIN(B18:B117)
123	Standard Deviation	=STDEV.S(B18:B117)
124	# below 0	=COUNTIF(B18:B117,"<0")

Table 11　Statistics formulas view

Table 10 shows that if 2,000 of the items are ordered, on average $2,550 was made in profit, at maximum $10,000, and at minimum a $5,000 loss. Also, 14 out of the 100 resulted in a profit of less than zero or a 14% loss. Thus, the business person evaluating this venture must find a 14% chance of losing money an acceptable risk or this venture is not worth pursuing.

Evaluating the Risk of Healthcare Plan Pricing

When using an Excel workbook within your organization, it is a good idea to ensure that data is being entered and analyzed correctly. Even one simple mistake can make users question the accuracy of everything included within the spreadsheet model.

Business Background

County Line Insurance Agency wants you to analyze existing health insurance data and create a spreadsheet model that will be used to ensure customers are being charged the correct premium. If the company can determine competitive pricing for its policies, then it will be able to compete with Obamacare and the policies offered on www.HealthCare.gov. Additionally, management would like you to calculate the cost of lost profits. Management has provided some details about the business below. The worksheets included in the workbook are as follows.

- Model—Contains the spreadsheet model that will be used as inputs for the simulation.
- Simulation—Contains the simulation, sensitivity, and risk analyses.

Additional details include the following.

- The demand for each policy and agent commission structure have been entered and given to you by management.
- Profit and loss data.

Marginal Policy Cost per Customer	$ 3
Fixed Costs	
Low Risk Administrative Cost	$ 10,000
Standard Risk Administrative Cost	$ 25,000
High Risk Administrative Cost	$ 50,000
Processing Fee	$ 86
Policy Capacity	50,000
Claim Assessment	$ 6

Points of Concern

Although a workbook has been created for you, the workbook's design needs to be modified so that it is easier to use and has more functionality. For example, you will need to insert a nested IF function that will determine the discount a customer will receive. Think about how this will change the workbook's functionality and interface.

Business Requirements

Management would like you to analyze data, and then identify and quantify the relationships between the inputs and outputs. Currently, the insurance agents have a pricing tool kit, but corporate headquarters wants the agents to think beyond the pricing and help solve business problems. A predictive model that includes sensitivity and demand analyses can assist with this request from the corporate office. The spreadsheet model must include the following.

- Add the profit and loss data to the Model worksheet.
- On the Model worksheet, use formulas and functions to calculate the following.
  - For Claim Value or Risk, use the RAND function nested in a VLOOKUP function or a nested IF function that will randomize the selection of claims risks—Low, Standard, or High.
  - For Demand, using the value displayed in B18, create a VLOOKUP function that incorporates the RAND and INDIRECT functions or a nested IF function. Use the functions to randomize the risk value and return a reference indicated by the text value.
  - For Risk Level, use the RAND function nested in a VLOOKUP function that will randomize the selection of individual demand.
  - For Total Policies Underwritten, display the smallest value between the sum of the Demand and Risk Level or the Policy Capacity.
  - For Cancellation Vouchers Issued, display the larger value between the sum of the Demand and Risk Level minus the Policy Capacity or zero.
  - For Paid Revenue, find the smallest value between Demand and Policy Capacity and then multiply the value by the Processing Fee.
  - For Fixed Cost, use a nested IF function to display the Low Risk Administrative Cost if the value in cell B18 is Low, to display the Standard Risk Administrative Cost if the value in cell B18 is Standard, or to display the High Risk Administrative Cost if the value in cell B18 is High.
  - For Marginal Cost, multiply Total Policies Underwritten by Marginal Policy Cost Per Customer.
  - For Voucher Cost, multiply Cancellation Vouchers Issued by Claim Assessment.
  - For Total Revenue, reference Paid Revenue.
  - For Total Cost, use a function to total the following costs: Fixed, Marginal, and Voucher.
  - For Profit, subtract Total Cost from Total Revenue.
- Create a named range for the cumulative probability and risk of the Claims, Low Risk, Standard Risk, High Risk, Individual, and Family tables. Using formulas, calculate the Cumulative Probability for the Claims, Low Risk, Standard Risk, High Risk, Individual, and Family tables.
- On the Simulation worksheet, complete the following to insert a table that will function as the predictive model.
  - In range B8:E8, reference the appropriate cells on the Model worksheet.
  - Insert a data table that will simulate 250 iterations of the risk analysis.
- On the Simulation worksheet, use a formula or function to calculate the Revenue, Cost, and Profit based on the rows that are displaying in the table.
- On the Simulation worksheet, use a formula or function to calculate the Average Profit Per Policy Type based on the rows that are displaying in the table.
- On the Simulation worksheet, insert three different scatterplots that chart the Revenue, Cost, and Profit based on the rows that are displaying in the table.
- On a new worksheet named BoxWhisker, insert a box and whisker chart that plots the Profit of each type of Risk based on the rows that are displaying in the table.
- Use appropriate formatting, text labels, named ranges, and organization throughout the spreadsheet model.
- Add a new worksheet named Named Ranges and then paste the list of named ranges that are included in the workbook.

MANAGER'S EMPHASIS
Referencing a Blank Cell

If you reference any blank cell in a data table, it forces the data table to refresh the random number similar to pressing F9.

Provided File

Healthcare workbook
ex03Healthcare.xlsx

A snapshot of the insurance agency model.

Analysis Questions

1. How will the spreadsheet model help management make better decisions? How would the business benefit from being able to simulate information on a regular basis?
2. Describe how you incorporated appropriate formatting, text labels, named ranges, and organization throughout the spreadsheet model.
3. How does the simulation model control for conditions of uncertainty?
4. What is the purpose of assessing risk? Do you think that clients will ever pay too much money, possibly causing negative consequences for the insurance agency?
5. How could predictive models help underwriters work more efficiently?
6. Do you have any recommendations for future changes to the spreadsheet model that would better suit the insurance agency?

Deliverables

1. Submit the ex03Healthcare_LastFirst.xlsx workbook as directed by your instructor.
2. As directed by your instructor, submit the following.

   ex03Analysis_LastFirst.docx with your answers to the analysis questions.

   ex03Memo_LastFirst.docx to explain and document your solution.

   ex03Presentation_LastFirst.pptx to present your recommendations, concerns, and findings to the analysis questions.

   Post a video presentation to YouTube or other instructor-provided location with a duration of less than five minutes.

Checklist

- ☐ Named ranges are created and used throughout the spreadsheet model and pasted on a new worksheet.
- ☐ All functions are created and include appropriate formatting.
- ☐ All formulas are created and include appropriate formatting.
- ☐ Table is created correctly and includes appropriate formatting.
- ☐ Scatterplots are created, customized, and include appropriate formatting.
- ☐ Appropriate formatting, text labels, named ranges, and organization are used throughout the spreadsheet model.
- ☐ All analysis questions are answered thoroughly.
- ☐ The memo thoroughly explains and documents the solution.
- ☐ The PowerPoint presentation thoroughly presented recommendations, concerns, and findings to the analysis questions, including appropriate formatting.
- ☐ The YouTube video includes all required steps including appropriate formatting.
- ☐ All deliverables are completed and named correctly.

Key Terms

Cost of lost profits   62
Decision theory   61
Heuristic   60
Predictive modeling   62
Risk assessment   61
Risk mitigation   61
Sensitivity analysis   60
Simulation analysis   60

Determining Economic Order Quantity and Optimal Product Mix to Maximize Profits

Excel Case 4 | ## ADVANCED PROBLEM SOLVING CASES FOR MICROSOFT OFFICE 2016

REQUIRED SKILLS

1. Create information with formulas and functions
2. Create named ranges
3. Clean data using text functions
4. Create data tables
5. Use Scenario Manager
6. Create optimization models using Solver
7. Create and interpret a Solver Sensitivity Report

Business Dilemma

Developing Optimization Models for Revolution Bikes

Research & Development

Revolution Bikes is a retail store that sells bicycles and bike accessories. They also create custom bikes for professional cyclists and for persons with disabilities. Revolution Bikes would like to keep costs as low as possible. Reducing inventory holding costs and minimizing lost sales due to supply shortages can keep costs low. The owners of Revolution Bikes need your help to create a spreadsheet model that will determine the ideal order quantity of bike frames for their custom bikes to meet demand while minimizing inventory and ordering costs. You will also determine the point at which they should place the order to avoid shortages. In addition, you will create a Solver model to determine the optimal mix of custom and non-custom bikes as well as accessories to sell in order to maximize their monthly profits.

MANAGER'S ADVICE ON THIS CASE

"Estimating the economic order quantity and reorder point for raw materials is one way to reduce costs. Managers should be aware that since businesses are constantly changing that the EOQ and ROP may change over time and to keep an eye on demand and be sure the estimates are adjusted when necessary."

— Robert Waldron, Inventory Manager

File provided by the business:

 ex04Inventory.xlsx

Deliverable files:

 ex04Inventory_LastFirst.xlsx

ex04Analysis_LastFirst.docx

ex04Memo_LastFirst.docx

 ex04Presentation_LastFirst.pptx

ex04Video_LastFirst

Understanding Economic Order Quantity (EOQ)

Inventory models designed to determine the optimal order quantity to minimize costs have been around for decades. **Economic order quantity (EOQ)** is the optimal order quantity that minimizes total inventory holding costs and ordering costs. The formula for calculating EOQ was developed over a century ago by Ford Whitman Harris of Westinghouse Corporation, and manufacturers who have utilized it have been reaping the benefits ever since.

$$EOQ = \sqrt{\frac{2 * Annual\ Usage * Order\ Cost}{Annual\ Holding\ Cost\ per\ Unit}}$$

EOQ Formula Inputs

The inputs required for the EOQ formula are further explained below:

- **Annual usage** (demand) is expressed in units and is the known or forecasted demand for the product for one year.

- **Order cost** is often referred to as purchase cost or setup cost and is the sum of all fixed costs incurred each time the item is ordered.

- **Carrying cost** is often referred to as holding cost and is the cost associated with having inventory on hand. Carrying costs typically include the rent for the storage space, equipment, labor, insurance, security, and other direct expenses as well as opportunity costs. Carrying costs are typically estimated anywhere from one-third to one-half of the value of the inventoried item each year.

Consider the following input values to calculate EOQ:

- Annual Usage = 10,000 units

- Order Cost = $10

- Carrying Cost = $20

  In Excel, the SQRT function is used to calculate the EOQ and would look like:
  = SQRT(2*10000*10/20)

The above formula results in an economic order quantity of 100 units. It is worth noting that an increase in the annual usage or ordering cost would increase the EOQ and an increase in holding cost would decrease the EOQ.

In order for the EOQ formula to provide the greatest benefit, there are a few necessary assumptions:

- The EOQ should be applied to only one product.

- The annual usage, known or forecasted, should be spread evenly throughout each month of the year.

- The ordering cost needs to be constant.

- **Lead time**, the delay between the initiation of the order and receipt of the order, is fixed.

- Restocking of inventory is done without delay, and products are delivered in complete batches.

- Purchase price is constant; for example, there are no discounts on purchased items.

Calculating a Reorder Point with Uncertain Demand

The standard EOQ inventory model assumes that demand for the product occurs at a constant rate. So, if annual demand for an item is 1,200, then monthly demand would be 100 units. As long as demand occurs at a relatively constant rate, then the EOQ formula is a good estimate to minimize inventory and ordering costs. However, demand is always uncertain, as no one can know for sure what the future holds.

When taking into consideration the uncertainty of demand in the context of inventory management, a useful question to ask is what the ideal reorder point is. **A reorder point (ROP)** is the level of inventory when an order should be made to bring the inventory levels up to the economic order quantity. When determining the optimal reorder point, the lead time must be taken into consideration. If future demand was known and supply was perfectly reliable, then the reorder point would simply be equal to the lead time demand. The **lead time demand (LTD)** is the forecasted demand during the lead time. An accurate estimate of the reorder point must also take into account any safety stock. **Safety stock** is the minimum level of inventory that is kept on hand to mitigate the negative effects of shortages due to fluctuations in demand. There are many different ways to determine the reorder point. One common way to calculate the Reorder Point is with the following formula:

$$Reorder\ Point = lead\ time\ demand + safety\ stock$$

If annual demand for a product is 5,000 and its lead time is 3 weeks, then the lead time demand is calculated by multiplying the annual demand by the lead time, in years.

LTD = 5,000 * (3/52), which is approximately 288.46. Add a safety stock of 120 to eliminate shortages and the reorder point is estimated to be 408.46.

It is worth noting that estimating how much safety stock to keep on hand is often very difficult. As a result, companies will often set a desired service level. **A service level** is the percentage of orders that you want to be able to fill on time. A 95% service level simply means that a company would like to be able to fill 95% of all orders without delay.

Optimizing Inventory and Maximizing Profits at Revolution Bikes

Revolution Bikes keeps an inventory of high-quality bike frames on hand for all their custom jobs and would like to minimize the holding costs and other expenses associated with excessive inventory and minimize the risk of losing any sales due to supply shortages. Also, since they sell both custom and standard bicycles, you have been asked to create a Solver model that will estimate the optimal number of each bike type to sell in order to maximize profits. They cannot produce more bicycles of either type than its estimated monthly demand nor can they use more resources than what is available.

Business Background

The owner of Revolution Bikes has provided you with an Excel spreadsheet containing the number of units sold each month over the last three years. This data will need to be cleansed before proceeding with the analysis. Below is the data necessary to calculate the EOQ and reorder point for the bike frames used in the custom builds.

- Annual demand is estimated as the average monthly units sold times 12.
- Each bike frame ordered costs $300.
- The cost to hold a unit in inventory for a year is $30.
- The lead time is always three weeks.
- Fifteen bike frames are always kept in inventory as part of the safety stock.

To assist you in building the model, Revolution Bikes has provided you with the information on the next page, including inputs and constraints.

MANAGER'S EMPHASIS

Clarity

Be sure to organize all the provided inputs logically to ensure the model is clear and easy to understand.

Costs

Hourly Wage	$12.10
Bike Frames (each)	$300
Aluminum (cost per oz.)	$0.75
Steel (cost per oz.)	$1.10
Plastic (cost per oz.)	$0.30

Resources Needed per Bike

	Custom	Standard
Labor (in hours)	15	2
Bike Frames	1	1
Aluminum (oz.)	10	4
Steel (oz.)	9	2
Plastic (oz.)	5	5

Materials and Production Constraints

Labor (hours)	325
Frames	60
Aluminum (oz.)	400
Steel (oz.)	300
Plastic (oz.)	350
Max Demand for Custom Bikes	27
Max Demand for Standard Bikes	40

Points of Concern

Revolution Bikes orders many different items from various suppliers and distributors. The economic order quantity can only be applied to a single item being ordered. Since bike frames are the most expensive product being purchased and stored in inventory, they are the focus of the EOQ. Because demand may vary from month to month, be sure the model is flexible by referencing cells instead of hardcoding in values for the formulas.

Business Requirements

See the list below for the basic requirements requested by the owner of Revolution Bikes. Be sure to label and format all values appropriately and use named ranges where appropriate.

- Calculate the economic order quantity, using the data provided in the ex04Inventory.xlsx worksheet and the data provided above.
- Calculate lead time demand by multiplying demand by lead time (converted to years; =3/52).
- Calculate the reorder point based on the lead time demand and safety stock.
- Create a one-variable data table to see how EOQ and the reorder point are affected when annual demand varies from 290–350 in increments of 10.

- Use the Scenario Manager to create a summary report showing the EOQ and reorder point for a worst-case, most-likely, and best-case scenario based on the following:
    - Worst-case: Demand = 300, Holding Costs = $45
    - Most-likely: Demand = 320, Holding Costs = $30
    - Best-case: Demand = 350, Holding Costs = $20
- On another worksheet, create a model that will use Solver to determine the number of custom and standard bikes to produce in order to maximize profits and stay within all material and production constraints.
- Create a Solver Sensitivity Report.

Provided File

Revolution Bikes' Monthly Units Sold ex04Inventory.xlsx	File contains data on units sold from 2015–2017

Analysis Questions

1. The data provided on the UnitsSold worksheet required some cleaning before it could be analyzed to calculate the estimated annual demand. What text functions did you use to clean the data? Explain how you knew which text functions to use.
2. What is the economic order quantity if annual demand is 320, order costs are $300, and holding costs are $30? Explain the business benefits of being able to calculate the EOQ.
3. Explain why estimating the reorder point further reduces costs for Revolution Bikes.
4. Interpret the results of the Scenario Summary and explain how it benefits the owners of Revolution Bikes.
5. Based on the results of your Solver model, how many custom bikes and standard bikes should be produced to maximize profits? What is the maximum profit that can be earned while not exceeding any of the defined constraints?
6. Based on the results of the Solver Sensitivity Report, which resource, if increased, would have the biggest impact on profit? How do you know this?

Deliverables

1. Submit the ex04Inventory_LastFirst.xlsx workbook as directed by your instructor.
2. As directed by your instructor, submit the following.

    ex04Analysis_LastFirst.docx with your answers to the analysis questions.

    ex04Memo_LastFirst.docx to explain and document your solution.

    ex04Presentation_LastFirst.pptx to present your recommendations, concerns, and findings to the analysis questions.

    Post a video presentation to YouTube or other instructor-provided location with a duration of less than five minutes.

Checklist

☐ EOQ, lead time demand, and ROP are calculated correctly.

☐ A one-variable data table is created to show the impact that changing demand has on EOQ and ROP.

☐ A Scenario Summary report is created showing the impact of EOQ and ROP in worst-case, most-likely, and best-case scenarios.

☐ Solver model lists costs for materials and labor clearly.

☐ Solver model lists resources needed to produce custom and standard bikes.

☐ Solver model includes calculations for revenue, costs, and profits based on the number of custom and standard bikes produced.

☐ Solver model clearly indicates the constraints on production of the bikes.

☐ Solver model produces an optimal solution for the product mix that maximizes monthly profits.

☐ A Solver Sensitivity Report is generated.

☐ All analysis questions are answered thoroughly.

☐ The memo thoroughly explains and documents the solution.

☐ The PowerPoint presentation thoroughly presents recommendations, concerns, and findings to the analysis questions, including appropriate formatting.

☐ The YouTube video includes all required steps including appropriate formatting.

☐ All deliverables are completed and named correctly.

Key Terms

Creating and Analyzing a Financial Business Plan

Excel Case 5 | ## ADVANCED PROBLEM SOLVING CASES FOR MICROSOFT OFFICE 2016

REQUIRED SKILLS

1. Construct a loan analysis with PMT, RATE, and NPER

2. Calculate cumulative interest and principal using CUMIPMT and CUMPRINC

3. Analyze investments using NPV and IRR

4. Calculate the depreciation of assets using SLN and DB

5. Conduct a basic statistical analysis using Data Analysis

6. Predict outcomes using probability distribution functions

7. Find relationships using COVARIANCE.S and CORREL

Business Dilemma

Creating and Analyzing a Financial Business Plan

Research & Development

Chloe Jants is fulfilling her long-term dream of opening a coffee shop on a busy corner of her hometown. Her town is like many others in the southern half of the state, and she has done a substantial amount of research regarding sales and customer patterns. Chloe has developed a startup plan with costs and expenses and would like to explore different loan options to see which would work best for her. She would also like to run a statistical analysis on the sales and customer patterns for which she has collected data.

MANAGER'S ADVICE ON THIS CASE

"Financial analysis of a business plan is far from an exact science. There are a lot of variables to take into account as well as a lot of unknown variables. Much of the analysis is based on industry standards and competition, which may or may not align with the coffee shop's vision as presented in this plan. All analysis should be done understanding that the results do not guarantee any specific results but will only be a guideline for us to make final decisions in the planning of the new coffee shop."

— Kaleb Hartz, silent partner in Chloe's Coffee Shop

File provided by the business:

 ex05Coffee.xlsx

Deliverable files:

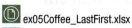 ex05Coffee_LastFirst.xlsx

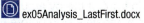 ex05Analysis_LastFirst.docx

ex05Memo_LastFirst.docx

 ex05Presentation_LastFirst.pptx

ex05Video_LastFirst

Analyzing Loan Options and Business Statistics

Excel includes financial functions to use for business and personal analysis and financial management. These financial functions are designed to calculate the monthly payment and other components of a loan, determine the future value of an investment, compare and contrast different investment opportunities, and calculate the depreciation of assets over time.

Businesses have an enormous amount of data available to them, from prices of raw materials to the number of links clicked on the company website. With so much data so easily available, it is becoming increasingly important to understand how to use that data to make good, strategic decisions. Statistical methods can be used to analyze business data to support good decision making.

Constructing a Loan Analysis

Many businesses and individuals need to borrow money and need to know what the monthly payment will be; the payment amount is dependent on the loan terms—the principal amount, the interest rate, and the length of the loan. The **PMT function** can be used to calculate a payment amount based on constant payments and a constant interest rate. Payments on business loans, mortgages, car loans, or student loans can be calculated.

The PMT function requires three arguments: rate, nper, and pv. The **rate** argument is the periodic interest rate—the interest rate for the loan.

> ### Points of Concern
> The interest rate used in a PMT function must be the interest rate per period. That means a monthly payment must be calculated using a monthly interest rate (dividing the annual interest rate by 12), whereas a quarterly payment must be calculated using a quarterly interest rate (dividing the annual interest rate by 4). The only time an annual interest rate would be the interest rate per period is for a loan where a yearly payment (once a year) is made.

The **nper** argument is the total number of payments that will be made in order to pay the loan in full. The **pv** argument is the present value of the loan and is usually the loan amount. Two optional arguments are the **fv** argument, which is the future value of the loan, or the balance you want to reach after the last payment is made. The ultimate goal is to pay off a loan, so if this argument is left blank, Excel assumes that the future value is zero. The **type** argument indicates when the payments are due—either at the beginning (1) or end (0) of a period. If the argument is left blank, Excel assumes the value is zero and the payment will occur at the end of the period.

Each loan payment in an amortized loan is made up of a principal amount and an interest amount. **Amortize** refers to repaying the balance of a loan over a period of time in multiple installments. The Cumulative Interest Payment function, or **CUMIPMT function**, can be used to calculate the amount of interest paid over a specific number of periods. The Cumulative Principal function, or **CUMPRINC function**, can be used to calculate the amount of principal paid over a specific number of periods.

> ### Points of Concern
> The CUMIPMT and CUMPRINC functions do not allow you to place a negative sign in front of the pv argument, so in order to display a positive result, you can place a negative sign before the function name.

Calculating NPV and IRR

One method of analyzing various investment opportunities is to compare the projected future cash flows generated from the investment to a risk-free investment, such as a bond. The Net Present Value function, or **NPV function**, is used to determine the value of an investment by analyzing a series of future incoming and outgoing cash flows expected to occur over the life of the investment. The function assumes that the cash flows occur at regular intervals, such as weekly, monthly, or quarterly, and measures the surplus or deficit of cash flows, in present value terms. This function is used for **capital budgeting**, the planning procedure used to evaluate whether an organization's long-term investments are worth pursuing. The discount rate used for the NPV calculation can be determined a number of different ways. One option is to decide the rate that the capital needed for the project could return if invested in a risk-free bond or other low-risk investment.

The Internal Rate of Return function, or **IRR function**, indicates the profitability of an investment and is commonly used in business when choosing between investments. This function is generally used in capital budgeting to measure and compare how profitable a potential investment is. The IRR of an investment is the rate that makes the net present value of both positive and negative cash flows equal to zero. In other words, the IRR function determines the discount rate at which you would break even on an investment.

Depreciating Assets

Businesses are required for tax and reporting purposes to show that the original cost of the property they purchase, such as buildings, vehicles, and equipment is reduced—or depreciated—over time as they "use up" these assets. When you depreciate the original cost of tangible assets, you first need to know the rules for depreciating the particular assets, because there are different rules for different types of assets. To calculate the depreciated value of an asset, you need to know the original cost of the asset, the asset's useful life, the asset's salvage value, and the rate at which the asset depreciates over time. Depreciation functions provide a method that matches the decline in value with the income that results from using the asset. To report the **net book value** of tangible assets, or the original cost of the asset minus the depreciation and amortization, a **depreciation schedule** must be maintained. The depreciation schedule will record the date the asset was placed into service, a calculation for each year's depreciation, and the accumulated depreciation.

One way you can calculate depreciation is by using the Straight-Line Depreciation function, or **SLN function**. The SLN function calculates the depreciation of an asset for one period using the fixed declining-balance method, which means the amount of money that is depreciated is the same for each year of the life of the asset. Another way you can calculate depreciation is by using the Declining-Balance function, or **DB function**. The DB function calculates the depreciation of an asset for a specified period using the fixed declining-balance method. The difference between the DB function and the SLN function is that when you use the DB function, you can specify the period and month that the asset was placed into service. Instead of spreading the cost of the asset evenly over its life as you did with SLN, the DB function calculates the depreciation of the asset at an accelerated rate, which results in higher depreciation in earlier periods and progressively declining depreciation each succeeding period.

Functions used for analyzing loan options and calculating depreciation.

- Payment function: =PMT(rate,nper,pv,[fv],[type])
- Rate function: =RATE(nper,pmt,pv,[fv],[type],[guess])
- Number of Periods function: =NPER(rate,pmt,pv,[fv],[type])
- Cumulative Interest Payment function:
  =CUMIPMT(rate,nper,pv,start_period,end_period,type)
- Cumulative Principal Payment function:
  =CUMPRINC(rate,nper,pv,start_period,end_period,type)
- Net Present Value function: =NPV(rate,value1,[value2],...)
- Net Present Value calculation: =NPV(rate,value1,[value2],...)+initial investment
- Internal Rate of Return function: =IRR(values,[guess])
- Straight-Line Depreciation function: =SLN(cost,salvage,life)
- Fixed-Declining Balance Depreciation function: =DB(cost,salvage,life,period,[month])

Applying Basic Statistical Methods and Using Descriptive Statistical Analysis

Statistics can be used to determine effectiveness of advertising campaigns, to understand what factors contribute to the demand for your products, to spot seasonal trends in the sales of certain products, and much more. Statistics often refer to populations and samples. In statistics, a **population** is defined as an entire collection of people, animals, plants, or anything on which you may collect data. Because businesses rarely have access to populations, a **sample population** or subset of a population is often used instead. More importantly, statistics rely heavily on **random samples**, or a subset of a population that has been selected using methods where each element of the population has an equal chance of being selected.

Three of the most basic descriptive statistics are mean, median, and mode. Each of these calculations attempts to define the **central tendency** of a data set. The central tendency refers to the way in which data tends to cluster around a value. The **mean** is the average of all the variables in a sample. The **median** describes which value falls in the middle when all the values of the sample are sorted in ascending order. The **mode** is the value that appears most often in a sample.

Calculations of the range, variance, and standard deviation of a data set are all methods used to determine the dispersion of a data set. Knowing how a data set is dispersed can provide a better understanding of the data than the mean, median, and mode alone. The **range** is the difference between the highest and lowest values in the data set. The **variance** determines how far the data set varies from the mean. The range can be determined by using the variance function or by calculating the minimum (MIN) and maximum (MAX) values and subtracting the two. The **standard deviation** is the most commonly used method for determining the average spread of a data set from the mean. Mathematically, the standard deviation is calculated by taking the square root of the variance.

Functions used in statistical analysis.

- Average (mean) function: =AVERAGE(number1,[number2],...)
- Median function: =MEDIAN(number1,[number2],...)
- Mode function: =MODE.SNGL(number1,[number2],...)
- Variance of a sample set of data function: =VAR.S(number1,[number2],...)
- Standard deviation of a sample set of data function: =STDEV.S(number1,[number2],...)
- Minimum function: =MIN(number1,[number2],...)
- Maximum function: =MAX(number1,[number2],...)

For more statistical analysis, the Analysis ToolPak add-in program can be added to the Excel ribbon. Descriptive statistics can be automatically generated on a range of data using the Analysis ToolPak.

Another useful calculation for a business that wishes to track sales or customers over time is called a **moving average**. A moving average calculates the average of values over time based on specified intervals. Moving average data can be used to create charts that show whether the value is trending upward or downward.

Applying Probability Distributions and Finding Data Relationships

Business professionals who use statistical analysis to support their decision making rely heavily on **probability distributions**. A probability distribution describes all the possible values and likelihoods that a given variable can be within a specific range. The distribution can be in the form of a chart, table, or formula.

A **normal distribution** is one of the most important distributions in statistics. When charted, it takes on the shape of a bell, where 98% of all values occur within three standard deviations from the mean. The normal distribution has wide applications in business and can be used to calculate the probability of sales, the number of customers to expect in a given week, employee performance, and operations, to name a few. The Normal Distribution function, or **NORM.DIST function**, can be used to calculate the probability of an event occurring by using the mean and standard deviation of a continuous variable data set, assuming the data follows a normal distribution.

To create a chart to visualize the normal distribution, the probability of values occurring within four standard deviations of the mean, both positive and negative, must be determined.

Identifying relationships in data can help answer questions that might arise from the probability distributions that predict the likelihood that certain events will occur. The **covariance** is a formula that can calculate the relationships between two variables, like age and dollars spent, as well as the direction of the relationship. If one variable increases and the other variable also increases, then the relationship is considered positive. If one variable increases and the other variable decreases, then the relationship is considered negative.

Another measure of the relationship between two variables is the **correlation coefficient**. The correlation coefficient is a value between −1 and 1 that describes the strength and direction of a relationship between two variables. A correlation coefficient of −1 is said to have a perfect negative relationship, a coefficient of 0 is said to have no linear relationship, and a coefficient of 1 is said to have a perfect positive relationship. The Covariance function, COVARIANCE.S, is used to determine the relationship between two variables in a sample set of data. Once the correlation coefficient values are calculated, they can be charted to illustrate the relationship between the variables.

Creating and Analyzing a Financial Business Plan

A new business requires more than passion and a good idea. A well thought out business plan with detailed financial analysis will not only help the owner objectively analyze his or her idea from a financial perspective, but will also enable the owner to secure financing from other sources. When approaching investors for startup money, they are going to look for financial information that will help them determine the level of risk involved in making the investment. While every investor and bank will have a different tolerance for risk and therefore different thresholds for making an investment, a detailed financial analysis will help them and the owner determine a good match for risk and return.

Business Background

Chloe knows that before she can put together a solid business plan for her coffee shop, she needs to analyze the data she already has. Some of the data includes estimates she came up with herself, like the start-up costs, while some of the data came from existing coffee shops in other similar areas, like the weekly and monthly statistics.

Business Requirements

Chloe has determined her start-up requirements for the coffee shop to be $218,000 and has divided these requirements into two categories: required expenses and required assets. The required total expenses include consulting fees ($4,500), architectural design ($12,500), building equipment ($24,000), and miscellaneous operations ($75,000). Her estimated required assets include cash ($45,000), property ($20,000), and miscellaneous assets ($37,000). With the total amount of expenses and assets covered, Chloe thinks she can get the coffee shop operational.

Loan Analysis

In order to acquire the money to cover her expenses and assets, Chloe has inquired at multiple banks and found the best annual interest rate she can secure for a start-up business loan is 7.2%. She would like to pay back her loan in 10 years. She would like to know what her monthly payments would be, both at the beginning and end of the period. Ideally, she would like to maintain a monthly payment of $2,200, so if the first payment calculation is more than that, she would like to see what rate, at both the beginning and end of the period, would ensure her a $2,200 monthly payment. Chloe knows she cannot secure a loan lower than 7.2% annually, so if the rate at a $2,200 payment is less than that, she would like to know how many years it would take at 7.2% to make monthly payments of $2,200. Finally, as a comparison, she would like to see the quarterly payments at 7.2% for 10 years, along with a breakdown of the principal and interest for each period and the total cumulative interest and total cumulative principal payments.

This analysis should be on a new worksheet called LoanAnalysis.

NPV Analysis

Chloe has an ambitious growth plan for her coffee shop and expects the following cash flows for the first 10 years:

Year 1	$10,000.00
Year 2	$12,300.00
Year 3	$15,100.00
Year 4	$18,600.00
Year 5	$22,800.00
Year 6	$28,100.00
Year 7	$34,600.00
Year 8	$42,500.00
Year 9	$52,400.00
Year 10	$64,400.00

She has determined her discount rate to be 3.5% and would like to know the net present value and internal rate of return using the total expenses and assets as her initial investment. This analysis should be on a new worksheet called NPV.

Depreciation Expense

The building equipment Chloe plans to purchase will have to be depreciated. She knows the salvage value of the equipment is $9,000 and the useful life is five years. She would like to see depreciation schedules showing the depreciation expenses for each year, the accumulated depreciation at the end of each year, and the book value at the end of each year. She would like to compare the depreciation schedules using both the straight-line depreciation method and the declining-balance depreciation method. This analysis should be on a new worksheet called Depreciation.

Statistical Analysis

Chloe has collected sample data on the number of customers who visit a successful coffee shop in a neighboring town for each day of the month. This data can be found on the DailyStats worksheet. She would like to see a moving average for every seven days, along with a chart that compares the number of customers each day with the moving average. She would also like to see the mean, median, mode, minimum, maximum, range, variance, and standard deviation values. She would also like to see the Descriptive Statistics calculated using the Data Analysis tool as a comparison. These statistics should be on a new worksheet called DescriptiveStatistics.

Chloe also collected, from the same neighboring coffee shop, the total number of customers who visit each month. This data can be found on the MonthlyStats worksheet. She would like to see the average and standard deviation for this data. Then based on a minimum number of customers each month of 7,100, Chloe would like to see a monthly customer distribution chart based on a normal distribution model.

Data Relationships

Chloe was able to find a sample distribution of the number of visits per customer by age. This data can be found on the Correlations worksheet. She would like to see the covariance and correlation between age and number of visits and also see a chart that illustrates this relationship.

Provided File

| Coffee Shop Sample Data | Worksheet with sample data. |
| ex05Coffee.xlsx | |

Analysis Questions

1. What difference does it make whether a payment is made at the beginning or end of a month?
2. Looking at the NPV and IRR results you just calculated, what would your recommendation be to Chloe? Would this be a good investment for her to make? Why or why not?
3. Explain why the two different depreciation methods result in different depreciation schedules. What would you recommend for Chloe and why?
4. What do the moving average calculations on the number of customers each day tell Chloe? What do the other statistics tell her? How can this data help her make decisions about daily operations?
5. What does the monthly customer distribution tell Chloe? How can she use this for strategic decision making?
6. What do the correlation calculations between age and number of visits tell Chloe? How can this data help her plan her daily operations?

Deliverables

1. Submit the ex05Coffee_LastFirst.xlsx workbook as directed by your instructor.
2. As directed by your instructor, submit the following.

   📄 ex05Analysis_LastFirst.docx with your answers to the analysis questions.

   📄 ex05Memo_LastFirst.docx to explain and document your solution.

   📄 ex05Presentation_LastFirst.pptx to present your recommendations, concerns, and findings to the analysis questions.

   ▶ Post a video presentation to YouTube or other instructor-provided location with a duration of less than five minutes.

Checklist

☐ The LoanAnalysis worksheet contains an analysis of four different loan options.

☐ The NPV worksheet shows an NPV analysis for Years 1 through 10.

☐ The Depreciation worksheet contains two depreciation schedules comparing the straight-line method and the declining-balance method.

☐ The DailyStats worksheet shows the moving average for the number of customers per day of the month and an appropriate chart of the moving average.

☐ The DescriptiveStatistics worksheet shows a descriptive statistics summary run from the Analysis ToolPak add-in.

☐ The MonthlyStats worksheet calculates the standard deviation of the monthly customer statistics and charts the monthly customer normal distribution.

☐ The Correlations worksheet shows the correlation between customer age and visits per month, including a chart.

☐ All charts, tables, and calculations are clearly named and labeled appropriately.

☐ All analysis questions are answered thoroughly.

☐ The memo thoroughly explains and documents the solution.

☐ The PowerPoint presentation thoroughly presents recommendations, concerns, and findings to the analysis questions, including appropriate formatting.

☐ The YouTube video includes all required steps including appropriate formatting.

☐ All deliverables are completed and named correctly.

Key Terms

Amortize   76
Capital budgeting   77
Central tendency   78
Correlation coefficient   79
Covariance   79
CUMIPMT function   76
CUMPRINC function   76
DB function   77
Depreciation schedule   77
fv   76
IRR function   77

Mean   78
Median   78
Mode   78
Moving average   79
Net book value   77
Normal distribution   79
NORM.DIST function   79
nper   76
NPV function   77
PMT function   76
Population   78

Probability distribution   79
pv   76
Random sample   78
Range   78
rate   76
Sample population   78
SLN function   77
Standard deviation   78
type   76
Variance   78

Identify Business Trends and Visualize Data with Dashboards

Excel Case 6 | ## ADVANCED PROBLEM SOLVING CASES FOR MICROSOFT OFFICE 2016

REQUIRED SKILLS

1. Create information with formulas and functions

2. Use Power Query and the Excel Data Model

3. Generate descriptive statistics with Excel functions

4. Create PivotTables and PivotCharts based on the Excel Data Model

5. Incorporate form controls into spreadsheets

6. Create KPIs and/or Power View reports

Business Dilemma

Developing a Competitive Strategy for Orchard Lawn Care

Research & Development

Matt Thomas founded Orchard Lawn Care in 2013 after graduating from college. Orchard Lawn Care is a specialty store that sells lawn mowers, a variety of trimmers, and other lawn care products. At first, Matt thought his business would specialize mostly in fertilizers and other lawn care chemicals. However, the region around his business soon grew quickly and the demand for lawn equipment has increased. Matt wants your help in analyzing some data from the past few years to gain a better understanding of the products he is selling and the customers purchasing the products. In addition to this analysis, you will build a digital dashboard so that Matt can monitor his sales and customers in real time.

MANAGER'S ADVICE ON THIS CASE

"Understanding what products our customers want, and at what time of year they want them, allows us to provide a more personal experience. With the ability to track our sales and goals in real time, we will be able to gain valuable insights into the operations of our business."

—Matt Thomas, Owner

Files provided by the business:

 ex06OrchardData.xlsx

 ex06Products.csv

 ex06Customers.csv

ex06OrchardTransactions.accdb

Deliverable files:

 ex06OrchardData _LastFirst.xlsx

 ex06Analysis_LastFirst.docx

ex06Memo_LastFirst.docx

 ex06Presentation_LastFirst.pptx

 ex06Video_LastFirst

Determining a Competitive Strategy

A **competitive strategy** is an organization's long-term plan to distinguish itself from various competitors in order to gain a competitive advantage. Competitive strategies are essential to organizations that operate in an industry where there are many alternatives for consumers. The objective is to increase demand for the goods and services offered by the organization. It is important to note that a competitive strategy is not just about marketing or publicity tactics. It also involves evaluating business processes and making changes where necessary.

The first step in determining a competitive strategy for an organization is to assess the fundamental characteristics and structure of the industry in which the organization resides. One framework used to assess an industry is Porter's Five Forces.

Porter's Five Forces

Porter's Five Forces is a framework developed by Harvard professor Michael Porter that identifies the five competitive forces that determine the state of competitiveness in an industry. These five forces also influence the profitability of organizations already in the industry. Whether or not the strength of each force is high or low determines the characteristics of the industry, how profitable it is, and how sustainable the profitability will be. Figure 1 lists each of the five forces in the Porter's Five Forces framework.

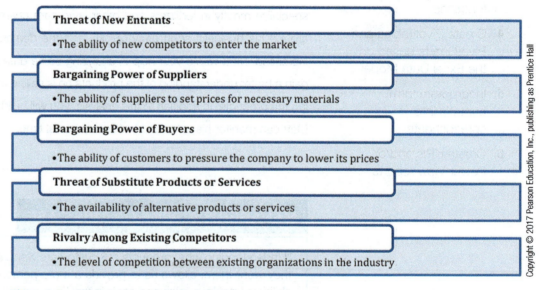

Threat of New Entrants
- The ability of new competitors to enter the market

Bargaining Power of Suppliers
- The ability of suppliers to set prices for necessary materials

Bargaining Power of Buyers
- The ability of customers to pressure the company to lower its prices

Threat of Substitute Products or Services
- The availability of alternative products or services

Rivalry Among Existing Competitors
- The level of competition between existing organizations in the industry

Figure 1 Porter's Five Forces

Once the strength of each force is determined, the organization must decide how it will respond to each force in order to weaken the strong forces and take advantage of the weak ones. Consider the lawn care products industry and the strength of each force that Matt Thomas must consider in order to increase the profitability of Orchard Lawn Care.

Threat of New Entrants:

Markets that are profitable and yield high returns will generally attract new entrants and eventually decrease the profitability of all firms in the industry. Some factors that can affect the strength of this force are as follows:

- Starting costs
- Government regulations

- Large established companies taking advantage of economies of scale
- Expected retaliation

Consider a small corner latte stand in the city; the starting costs are relatively low to purchase the equipment and obtain the required business license. There are minimal government regulations to create barriers to entry, and although there are most likely large competitors in the area capable of retaliating, they are unlikely to see a corner latte stand as a threat. These factors will make the threat of new entrants fairly strong in terms of other small corner latte stands.

Bargaining Power of Suppliers:

When there are few to no alternatives, suppliers of raw materials, labor, services, and so on can have power over the organizations that rely on those resources. Some factors that can affect the strength of this force are the following:

- Number of suppliers
- Size of suppliers
- Available substitutes
- Cost of changing suppliers

Consider a cable provider as a supplier of high-speed internet and VoIP phone service to businesses; since there are very few players in the industry, the cable providers have a lot of power over prices, offerings, and quality of service. This often results in higher prices for consumers without the benefit of better quality.

Bargaining Power of Buyers:

A customer's buyer power can be strong if an organization has only a few powerful customers who are able to bring down the price of a product or service. For most consumer products, the individual's buyer power is low. However, giant retail stores have more buyer power and are able to negotiate a lower cost when buying large quantities. Some factors that can affect the strength of this force are as follows:

- Number of customers
- Size of each order
- Available substitutes
- Differences among competitors

If you consider consumer-based products, an individual customer's buyer power is low because customers are fragmented and have very little influence on the price of products. However, if you consider large retail stores as the buyers instead of individuals, then the firms providing the products face strong buyer power because large retail stores can take advantage of economies of scale. **Economies of scale** is an economics term that refers to the notion that large organizations can reduce the per-unit costs of an item by being able to purchase large quantities of that item.

Threat of Substitute Products or Services:

A substitute is a product that provides the same or similar function as another product. The more substitutes a product or service has, the more that demand for that product becomes elastic. This means that consumers are more sensitive to prices and are more likely to seek out substitutes if prices increase. Some factors that can affect the strength of this force are the following:

- Quality of substitutes
- Price difference of substitutes
- Cost associated with switching to a substitute

Consider the oil and gas industry; although substitutes, in terms of alternative energy sources, are being researched and introduced into the market, most vehicles rely heavily on gasoline for fuel. This creates a weak threat of substitute products in this industry.

Rivalry Among Existing Competitors:

For most industries the strength of this force is what determines the overall competiveness and therefore profitability of an industry. Some factors that can affect the strength of this force are as follows:

- Number of competitors
- Quality differences
- Customer loyalty

Consider the smartphone manufacturing industry; Apple, Samsung, HTC, and Nokia are the major key players in the industry. These companies are in intense competition with each other in an attempt to gain more market share by lowering costs, creating innovative designs, and promoting their products with an increase in advertising and promotions.

Porter's Four Competitive Strategies

According to Michael Porter, organizations respond to the structure of the industry, as determined by Porter's Five Forces, by developing a competitive strategy. According to Porter, organizations engage in one of four competitive strategies (see Figure 2). An organization can compete on cost and become a cost leader, or it can focus on differentiating its products from the competition in some way. An organization can deploy either strategy across an entire industry or focus its strategy on a particular segment of the industry.

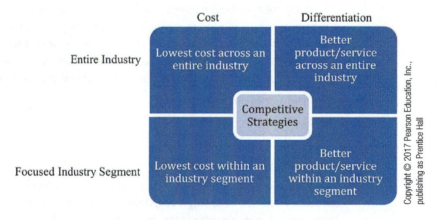

Figure 2   Porter's Four Competitive Strategies

Orchard Lawn Care sells a variety of lawn equipment ranging from push mowers to riding mowers to gas- and electric-powered equipment. Matt Thomas would like to develop an understanding of what types of equipment his customers are buying so that he can better maintain inventory at his store and minimize the need for customers to special order their equipment. Importantly, Matt is curious if there is a seasonal trend to sales at his store. Given his location in the Midwest of the United States, he is interested in identifying if there is a notable increase or decrease in sales of products during distinct seasons. Additionally, he is curious about whether, over the past year, the store has been selling more electric-powered products than gas-powered products. Matt has supplied you with some data about the products, customers, and sales at the store to begin your analysis.

Business Background

Matt Thomas has provided you with an Excel spreadsheet containing a monthly summary of sales over the past three years. Additionally, you have been provided with exports of data from the store's purchasing system. The data includes two CSV exports, one listing product names and prices and another listing customers and their ages. Lastly, you have been given an Access database that is tracking purchases of the products Matt wants to analyze. The transactions begin in 2014 and span through 2016.

Points of Concern

The Data Analysis Add-ins are not enabled in Excel by default. To enable them, click File, Options, and then Advanced. Scroll down to the Data group and select the Enable Data Analysis Add-ins: Power Pivot, Power View, and Power Map check box.

Business Requirements

Matt Thomas wants to better understand any patterns of sales occurring at Orchard Lawn Care. He has requested that you build an analysis of the monthly sales summary he has provided you and also build a dashboard that will allow him to track seasonal sales and sales goals of the business in real time. The analysis must include the following:

- Complete the following tasks on the MonthlySales worksheet:
    - Use the Data Analysis ToolPak to calculate a moving average of Total Sales for every month. Include a chart to visualize the results along with a forecast line.
    - Calculate the Mean, Median, Min, Max, Range, and Sample Standard Deviation of the monthly sales data in column C.
    - Using the data in column C, create a box and whisker plot to analyze the distribution of sales in the three-year sample.
- Import and create relationships for the data for the dashboard by completing the following tasks:
    - Add the ex06Products CSV file to the workbook's data model using Power Query. Before loading the data to the Data Model, capitalize the first letter of each word in the Product Name field and change the data type of the Price field to Currency.
    - Add the ex06Customers CSV file to the workbook's data model using Power Query.
    - Add the tblTransactions table from the Access database to the workbook's data model using Power Query. Before loading the data to the Data Model, transform the Date column to Date Only, and extract the year into a new column.
    - Create relationships between the three tables in Power Pivot using the appropriate fields.
- On the Dashboard worksheet, create the dashboard Matt has requested that includes the following:
    - A PivotChart that displays both the sales revenue and number of transactions for all three years of data in tblTransactions.
    - Calculate the quarterly sales for the entire store in a table.
        - Include a spin button that will change the year beginning with 2014 and ending at 2016.
        - The table should list each quarter individually for the year displayed by the spin button.

- A PivotTable showing the number of items sold and the total sales of each item by Year and Category.
- Create a Timeline slicer that filters by year and a slicer that filters by product name. Attach both slicers to the PivotChart and the PivotTable.
- Matt wants to set a goal of a 10% increase in sales for each product from the prior year. Create a KPI for 2016 sales. The KPI should be based on the sales for 2015 and have a low threshold of 100% and a high threshold of 110%.
- Create a second PivotTable that shows the 2016 sales KPI by Product Name and Category. Include the 2016 Sales Values, Goal, and Status in the PivotTable.

- Clean up the dashboard by hiding the gridlines as well as the column and row headings.
- Ensure that the use of the slicers does not result in the contents of cells becoming obscured or displaying as # symbols.
- Protect the Dashboard worksheet, ensuring that the filters and form controls can still be used.
- Be sure to keep any necessary analysis that is not part of the dashboard on a separate worksheet in the workbook.

Provided Files

Orchard Lawn Care's data	
ex06Customers.csv	Listing of customers provided by Orchard Lawn Care.
ex06OrchardData.xlsx	Business data provided by Orchard Lawn Care for use in your analysis.
ex06OrchardTransactions.accdb	Table of transactions provided by Orchard Lawn Care.
ex06Products.csv	Listing of products provided by Orchard Lawn Care.

Analysis Questions

1. Conduct an analysis of the lawn care products industry for Orchard Lawn Care using Porter's Five Forces framework. Evaluate each of the forces and determine whether each force is strong or weak.
2. Based on your analysis, what do you recommend Orchard Lawn Care focus on in terms of its competitive strategy?
3. Based on your analysis, are there any seasonal patterns in the data? Describe these patterns. What recommendations would you have for Orchard Lawn Care?
4. Is there a significant difference in the type of electric- versus gas-powered items sold by Orchard Lawn Care?
5. Based on the moving average analysis, what can you say about the sales at Orchard Lawn Care?
6. As a part of this analysis, you connected the spreadsheet to multiple data sources. Discuss the benefits of creating links to these data sources as opposed to copying and pasting the data into a worksheet directly.

Deliverables

1. Submit the ex06OrchardData_LastFirst.xlsx workbook as directed by your instructor.
2. As directed by your instructor, submit the following.

    ex06Analysis_LastFirst.docx with your answers to the analysis questions.

    ex06Memo_LastFirst.docx to explain and document your solution.

ex06Presentation_LastFirst.pptx to present your recommendations, concerns, and findings to the analysis questions.

Post a video presentation to YouTube or other instructor-provided location with a duration of less than five minutes.

Checklist

☐ Loaded ex06Products.csv to the Excel Data Model using Power Query with data transformed.

☐ Loaded ex06Customers.csv to the Excel Data Model.

☐ Loaded the tblTransactions table from the ex06OrchardTransactions Access database to the Excel Data Model with data transformed.

☐ MonthlySales worksheet contains Moving Average column with charted results.

☐ MonthlySales worksheet contains statistics and box and whisker chart.

☐ Connected all of the tables in the Data Model using appropriate relationships.

☐ PivotChart created to display sales revenue and number of transactions over time.

☐ Table created displaying Quarterly sales revenues by Year. Table includes a spin button to interact with the year.

☐ PivotTable created showing the items sold and total sales by year and category.

☐ KPI for 2016 sales created.

☐ PivotTable created incorporating the 2016 sales KPI.

☐ Dashboard worksheet has gridlines and column and row headings hidden.

☐ Dashboard worksheet is protected and allows for slicers and form controls to be used.

☐ All analysis questions are answered thoroughly.

☐ The memo thoroughly explains and documents the solution.

☐ The PowerPoint presentation thoroughly presents recommendations, concerns, and findings to the analysis questions, including appropriate formatting.

☐ The YouTube video includes all required steps including appropriate formatting.

☐ All deliverables are completed and named correctly.

Key Terms

Bargaining power of buyers   87
Bargaining power of suppliers   87
Competitive strategy   86
Economies of scale   87
Porter's Five Forces   86
Rivalry among existing competitors   88
Threat of new entrants   86
Threat of substitute products or services   87

Linking Data for Advanced Analysis

Access and Excel Case 1

ADVANCED PROBLEM SOLVING CASES FOR MICROSOFT OFFICE 2016

REQUIRED SKILLS

1. Cleanse Excel data
2. Create a new Access table from Excel data
3. Import Excel data into Access
4. Link Access data to Excel
5. Save import steps
6. Create an Access report
7. Create an Excel chart
8. Create information with formulas and functions

Business Dilemma

Turquoise Oasis Spa's New Product Management

Production & Operations

Rodate Meda, manager of the Turquoise Oasis Spa, has just found out that the spa's largest vendor, Relaxation Creations, will start sending it detailed information on new products in an Excel spreadsheet once a month. Rodate does not think the Access database they currently use for product management will accommodate this new information easily, but she would like to continue using Access to keep track of her products. She would like you to use two recent files sent by Relaxation Creations to create a new database and decide the best way to add data to it each time a new file is received from Relaxation Creations. Rodate would also like you to consider how to create both charts and reports using this data in Access.

MANAGER'S ADVICE ON THIS CASE

"While linking Excel and Access data can be a time saver, it is critical to have the required steps documented so even those unfamiliar with the two programs can successfully complete the task. Updated procedures and documentation will make the process go smoother each time it has to be done and will help new and inexperienced users work with the programs. This documentation should be updated on a regular basis and given to a nonuser to preview to make sure it is easy to understand and follow."

— Aiden Matthews, Chief Technology Officer

Files provided by the business:

- i01AprilNew.xlsx
- i01MayNew.xlsx

Deliverable files:

- i01Products_LastFirst.accdb
- i01AprilNew_LastFirst.xlsx
- i01MayNew_LastFirst.xlsx
- i01NewProductLink_LastFirst.xlsx
- i01Analysis_LastFirst.docx
- i01Memo_LastFirst.docx
- i01Presentation_LastFirst.pptx
- i01Video_LastFirst

Exchanging Data Between Access and Excel

Data stored in either Access or Excel may require different types of manipulation depending on the goal of your analysis. You may want to work with Excel data in Access to take advantage of Access's reporting and querying functions. Or, you might want to use Excel's charting features with Access data. Sometimes a simple copy and paste of the data from one program to the other will suffice, but using the import, export, and link features of the two programs will often provide a more robust solution.

You cannot save an Excel workbook as an Access database. If you open an Excel workbook in Access, Access will create a link to the workbook instead of importing the data. Therefore, linking to a workbook is different than importing a worksheet into a database.

It is important to understand that the term "import" means two different things depending on whether you are talking about Access or Excel. In Excel, **importing** makes a permanent connection to data in Access that can be refreshed. In Access, importing brings data into Access without a permanent connection.

Depending on the situation, there are a number of methods to exchange data between the two programs.

QUICK REFERENCE	Exchanging Data

Transferring from Excel to Access: to bring data into Access from Excel

- Copy and paste – best for when data exchange is temporary
- Import an Excel worksheet into an Access table – best for when data exchange is periodic
- Link to an Excel worksheet from an Access table – best for regular exchange of data

Transferring data from Access to Excel: to bring data into Excel from Access

- Copy and paste – best for when data exchange is temporary
- Export data into an Excel worksheet – best for when data exchange is periodic
- Connect to an Access database from an Excel worksheet – best for regular exchange of data

Import Excel Data into Access

Often, you will have data in Excel and want to use Access features like forms and reports with that data. When you import data from Excel, Access will store this imported data in a new or existing table, whichever you specify. The data will not be connected to the Excel worksheet, so changes made in Access will not affect the data in Excel and vice versa. You can only import data from one worksheet at a time, so to import multiple sheets will require you to repeat the process multiple times.

In order to successfully import the data from Excel into Access, the data in Excel should be prepared for the import and meet the following guidelines:

- The cells to import must be in tabular format.

- The number of columns you import cannot exceed 255.

- Only rows or columns you want to import should be included in the worksheet or named range to import. All other data should be removed before the import.

- All blank columns and rows in the worksheet or named range to be imported should be deleted.

- Any cells with error values like #NUM or #DIV should be corrected before the import.

- Each column in the worksheet or named range should contain the same type of data in each row (text, number, etc.).

- Each column in the worksheet or named range should be assigned a specific data format before it is imported.

- If the first row of the worksheet or named range contains the names of the columns, you can specify that Access uses those names during the import.

- As much as possible, the data should be error free.

The Access database should be prepared for the import by meeting the following guidelines:

- If appending the Excel data to an existing table, the name and data type of each column must exactly match the corresponding fields. Also, the data need to match any input masks and be acceptable for any validation rules.

- If one or more fields in the worksheet do not exist in the destination table, those fields must be added.

- If the table contains a primary key field, that field must exist in the corresponding Excel worksheet and the values must be compatible with the primary key field.

Export Access Data to Excel

Working with Access data in Excel allows you to take advantage of Excel's data analysis and charting features. You can use the **Export Wizard** in Access to export an Access database object (table, query, or form) into an Excel worksheet. By using the wizard, you can save the export details to perform the same process on a regular basis and even schedule the export to run automatically at specified intervals.

Some things to know before you export data from Access to Excel:

- Fields that support multiple values are exported as a list of values separated by semicolons.

- Graphical objects (attachments and contents of OLE object fields) will not be exported and must be manually added to the worksheet after the export.

- Null values in the database may often be replaced by the data that should be in the next column.

- Dates earlier than January 1, 1900, are not exported and will show a null value in the cell.

- Expressions are not exported—only the results of the calculations are exported.

- A form should be opened in Datasheet view before exporting the data to prevent a # value in a Yes/No field.

Connect to Access Data from Excel

If you store your data in Access and would like to use the features in Excel to analyze the data, you can create a connection between Access and Excel for that data. The benefit of connecting the data rather than importing it is that you can automatically refresh, or update, the data in the Excel workbook from the original Access database whenever the database is updated.

Exchanging data this way involves importing data from Access into Excel. You can choose to import data from an Access table or query. You can choose to view the data as a table, a PivotTable report, or a PivotChart. And, you can choose to put the data in an existing worksheet or a new worksheet.

Note: Connections to external data might be disabled on your computer. If you want to connect to data when you open a workbook, either save the workbook in a trusted location or enable data connections by using the Trust Center bar. You may also need to refresh your data to get the most updated data. On the Data tab in Excel, in the Connections group, click Refresh All.

Link to Excel Data from Access

If you want to maintain your data in Excel but have it regularly available in Access as well, you can link the data. This type of link must be created from the Access database and not from Excel. This type of link creates a new table in Access that is linked to the Excel source cells. When the source cells in Excel change, the data in the linked Access table also changes. However, you cannot change the data in Access; all changes must be made in the Excel source cells. These cells may be a whole worksheet or only a named range.

Some things to remember when you are linking to Excel data:

- You cannot create a link to a database from within Excel; it must be done in Access.
- A new linked table will be created in Access but will NOT store the data in Access.
- You cannot link Excel data to an existing table in a database, which means you cannot append data to a table.
- Any changes you make in Excel are automatically shown in the linked table.
- If you open an Excel worksheet in Access, Access will create a blank database and automatically start the Link Spreadsheet Wizard.

To prepare the Excel data for the link, the same guidelines for importing Excel data should be followed.

Cleanse Excel Data to Prepare It for Linking and Importing

In addition to the guidelines above, data in Excel should be cleansed before it is imported or linked to an Access database. The nature of data is the data is dirty. Real-world data typically has all kinds of errors and inconsistencies. **Data cleansing** is the process of finding and fixing obvious errors. Data cleansing is not data verification. **Data verification** is the process of certifying that all data is accurate. For example, suppose you want to import phone numbers. Cleansing the phone numbers would look for phone numbers that do not have an area code or are in the incorrect format. To verify the data, you would call the phone number and verify it calls the correct person. Data verification is costly and time consuming. Thus, most companies cleanse the data. Cleansing prevents importing errors as well as making sure the data matches the table into which you are importing the data.

- Spell check—Use the spell checker to find misspelled words and values that are not used consistently. This can be done by adding unusual names to the dictionary.
- Remove duplicate rows—You can filter for unique values and then remove any duplicate values.
- Find and replace text—Use Find and Replace or various functions (FIND, REPLACE, etc.) to find and remove unnecessary data.
- Change the case of text—Convert text to lowercase or uppercase for consistency by using functions such as LOWER, PROPER, or UPPER.
- Remove spaces and nonprinting characters—Trailing and leading space characters can interfere with sorting, filtering, and importing data. Using functions such as CLEAN, TRIM, or SUBSTITUTE can remove these characters.
- Fix numbers and number signs—If a number needs to be imported as text, or a negative sign needs to be changed, use a function like TEXT.
- Fix dates and times—Dates and times might have to be formatted to prevent confusion with other formats. Functions like DATE, DATEVALUE, or TIME may be used.
- Merge and split columns—In order to match columns between the source data and the destination table, columns may be split or combined using various functions such as CONCATENATE.
- Transform and rearrange rows—Rows and columns may be switched by using the Transpose option.

- Reconcile table data by joining or matching—To reconcile or compare tables from different worksheets to find duplicate data or rows that do not match, any number of lookup functions may be used (LOOKUP, HLOOKUP, VLOOKUP, etc.).
- New to Office 2016—Many of the data cleansing operations can be completed using Get & Transform.

Getting and Transforming Data in Excel

While shorter than data verification, the process of data cleansing can take a long time. When you want to pull data on a regular basis, the data needs to be cleansed every time. New to Office 2016, you can get the data from many types of outside sources including Access, SharePoint, Facebook, Salesforce, Hadoop, and many others. When you get the data in Excel, Excel creates a query. You can choose to store the data in Excel or link to the source. Inside the query, you can transform—or cleanse—the data. Excel saves each step of the transformation. Then, every time the data is refreshed, those same transformation steps are performed in the same order. This can be a huge time saver.

QUICK REFERENCE	Get & Transform Data

To use Get & Transform, on the Data tab, click New Query. Then, select From Database and then From Microsoft Access Database. Find and select the database file. Click Import. In the Navigator window, select the table from the database to import. By default, it will load the data to the worksheet currently selected.

If you just want to connect to the data, click the arrow next to Load and select Load To. Select where you want the data stored or choose Only Create Connection. Click Load. Then, you can hover over the query in the Workbook Queries pane that opens on the right. In the window that opens, click on Edit.

From the Edit screen, many types of transformations can be done. The transformations you make are recorded as Applied Steps in the Query Settings pane on the right. These steps will be performed on the data every time the data is refreshed.

Points of Concern

Dirty data leads to poor decisions! Data cleansing can be difficult and time consuming. However, if you don't take that time, you are likely to make poor or incorrect decisions.

QUICK REFERENCE	Sharing Data

How you want to share your data will determine the method you use. Some methods are better for sharing one time, while others are better for sharing on a regular basis.

Scenario	Method
You store your data in Access but like to use Excel for analysis for a one-time purpose.	Export Access data to Excel
You like to store your data in Access, but your boss likes to see the data in Excel. You want to automate the process of moving and cleansing the data.	Get & Transform the data in Excel from Access
You have data in Access that you update monthly and would like to chart in Excel on a regular basis.	Connect to Access data from Excel

Scenario	Method
You want to move your data from Excel to Access to start managing it exclusively in Access.	Import Excel data into Access
You occasionally receive data in an Excel format and it must be merged with your Access data.	Import Excel data into Access
Your data is stored in Access but you receive monthly or weekly updates in Excel and would like to automate the process of moving the data to Access.	Import Excel data into Access and Save the Import Steps
You maintain your data in Excel but would like to use features in Access on a regular basis.	Link to Excel data from Access

Linking Data for Advanced Analysis

Some people prefer working in Excel, while others prefer working in Access. Both programs are exceptional programs to use to maintain your data, but they each have their own strengths, so by using both, you can optimize data analysis. Importing data will allow you to exchange data on a temporary basis, as it will have to be updated manually if the source data changes. Linking or connecting the data will allow for a somewhat seamless connection between the two programs, which allows you to harness the best of both programs.

Business Background

Rodate Meda, manager at the Turquoise Oasis Spa, has provided you with two inventory files provided by their biggest supplier, Relaxation Creations. These files are in Excel format and contain the following fields: Date, ProductName, ProductDescription, Category, WholesaleCost, MinOrderQty, Size, Units, and Color. She has noticed that occasionally there are spelling errors in the data, the vendor inserts blank rows between different types of products, capitalization is inconsistent, and some cells have non-printable characters—such as extra spaces and hard returns. The file is not quite ready for the Access database she is expecting.

Points of Concern

When sharing data between Excel and Access, there are a variety of options depending on your desired results. Some options will be more appropriate for long-term linking and others more appropriate for one-time linking. You will need to determine which methods work best for the results that are being requested. You should keep in mind the end users, the frequency of the linking, and the desired end results of the linking when choosing the methods to use.

Business Requirements

Rodate would like to see a new database created using the files sent by Relaxation Creations. The first file sent for the 4/8/18 new product availability date should be used to create the new database. Rodate would like to see the following fields (in this order) in the Access database:

- ID (Access will assign as primary key field)
- AvailableDate
- Product (which will be a combination of the ProductName in proper case and the ProductDescription with a hyphen in between and can be created using the

CONCATENATE function in Excel). The Product should use proper case and have no non-printable characters.

- Category
- WholesaleCost
- RetailPrice (which will be a 50% markup over the purchase price rounded to the nearest penny)
- MinOrderQty
- Size
- Units
- Color

Because there are more fields required in the Access table than are in the Excel file, the Excel file will have to be prepared first before the data is shared with Access. Rodate is also concerned about the spelling errors, blank rows, inconsistent capitalization, and non-printable characters in the files from Relaxation Creations.

Once the new table is created in Access, a process will need to be set up to prepare the data and share it with Access on a regular basis. The second shipment file should be used to come up with this process. The new product data received from Relaxation Creations must be added to the same table in Access, so the available products can be tracked over time. Rodate would like this process documented, so it can be shared with all the spa employees.

After the data has been added to the Access database, Rodate would like a report grouped by category and sorted newest to oldest by AvailableDate to be able to easily see a list of products available to purchase.

To go along with this report, Rodate would also like to see a chart showing the average retail price of each category in Excel. This may be best accomplished by using a PivotTable and Chart. Since these charts will be done on a somewhat regular basis, Rodate thinks creating a link between Access and Excel might be the best option, so the data will be automatically refreshed when data is added to the Access database.

Provided Files

Turquoise Oasis Spa's Sales Data	
i01AprilNew.xlsx	File that was sent by Relaxation Creations for the April new products.
i01MayNew.xlsx	File that was sent by Relaxation Creations for the May new products.

Analysis Questions

1. Why is it so important to prepare the Excel data before it is added to Access? What other types of guidelines should be used? What other tools are available for cleansing the data?
2. Explain the step-by-step process you set up to prepare the data from the Excel new products file to add it to the products table in Access.
3. Why do you think Rodate prefers storing the products data in Access? What are the advantages to doing so? What are the disadvantages?
4. How will linking the Access data to Excel help the staff better manage their products? Why not just copy and paste the data between the two programs?
5. Why do you think businesses like to use Excel more than Access? What arguments would you make for using both?

Deliverables

1. Submit the i01Products_LastFirst.accdb database as directed by your instructor.
2. Submit the i01AprilNew_LastFirst.xlsx and i01MayNew_LastFirst.xlsx workbooks as directed by your instructor.
3. Submit the i01NewProductLink_LastFirst.xlsx workbook as directed by your instructor.
4. As directed by your instructor, submit the following.

   📄 i01Analysis_LastFirst.docx with your answers to the analysis questions.

   📄 i01Memo_LastFirst.docx to explain and document your solution.

   📄 i01Presentation_LastFirst.pptx to present your recommendations, concerns, and findings to the analysis questions.

   ▶ Post a video presentation to YouTube or other instructor-provided location with a duration of less than five minutes.

Checklist

☐ AprilNew and MayNew Excel files were prepared for uploading to Access.

☐ A new database was created using the AprilNew and MayNew Excel files.

☐ An Access report was created using the imported Excel data.

☐ An Excel chart was created using linked Access and Excel data.

☐ All analysis questions are answered thoroughly.

☐ The memo thoroughly explains and documents the solution.

☐ The PowerPoint presentation thoroughly presents recommendations, concerns, and findings to the analysis questions, including appropriate formatting.

☐ The YouTube video includes all required steps including appropriate formatting.

☐ All deliverables are completed and named correctly.

Key Terms

Data cleansing 96
Data verification 96
Export Wizard 95
Importing 94

Determine the Feasibility of a New System

Access and Excel Case 2 | ## ADVANCED PROBLEM SOLVING CASES FOR MICROSOFT OFFICE 2016

REQUIRED SKILLS

1. Cleanse Excel data
2. Create additional Access tables
3. Use Excel to normalize data
4. Create Access forms
5. Create Access queries
6. Create macros

Business Dilemma

Developing a Software Solution for Gaming Master

Production & Operations

Gaming Master is a local business that specializes in selling hand-selected, quality board games, card games, party games, and puzzles. It also hosts gaming competitions at its facility throughout the year. Daryl Dixon is the owner of Gaming Master and has been using an Access database to track events and event reservations, and an Excel worksheet to track sales. He would like a single system that can help him track both events and sales for Gaming Master. You have been asked to assist in developing a software solution.

MANAGER'S ADVICE ON THIS CASE

"Selecting an appropriate software system is a critical decision for an organization of any size. Conducting a thorough feasibility analysis will help to ensure that a good decision is made and that the system meets the needs and constraints of the organization."

— Gloria Franklin, Project Manager

Files provided by the business:

 i02SalesData.xlsx

 i02GamingMaster.accdb

Deliverable files:

 i02GamingMaster_LastFirst.accdb

 i02SalesData_LastFirst.xlsx

 i02Analysis_LastFirst.docx

 i02Memo_LastFirst.docx

 i02Presentation_LastFirst.pptx

 i02Video_LastFirst

Evaluating a New Software System

As competition intensifies in certain markets, it becomes increasingly more difficult to maintain existing customers and to attract new ones. One common response to this increased competitiveness is to develop a customer relationship management strategy. **Customer relationship management (CRM)** is a strategy that a company utilizes to initiate and manage the interactions with existing and future customers. **A CRM software system** is a suite of applications, a database, and a set of inherent processes that are used by the business to manage all interactions with its customers from lead generation to customer service.

Businesses may consider many other responses to increased competitiveness in an industry. **Supply chain management (SCM) software** refers to a wide range of software tools used to manage the interactions along the supply chain from procurement of materials to the sale of the finished product. An effective SCM implementation could result in lower costs, which can allow a company to compete as a cost leader in an intensely competitive market.

There are many different business needs that can be met with various software systems. **Application software** is a computer program that performs a specific task other than running the computer itself such as an operating system. The application components of CRM and SCM software systems, instant messengers, word processors, and spreadsheet software are all examples of application software. There are three different categories of application software: horizontal-market applications, vertical-market applications, and custom-developed applications.

Horizontal-Market Applications

Horizontal-market applications are general purpose applications that can be used across a variety of industries. Common examples of horizontal-market applications are word processors, presentation software, and photo editing software as they can be used by virtually any type of business or consumer.

Specific examples of this type of application are Microsoft Word, Access, Excel, and Adobe Photoshop. Each of these examples are used in a wide variety of businesses across all industries as well as in the consumer market. These applications are purchased off the shelf or downloaded from the publisher with little to no customization.

Vertical-Market Applications

Vertical-market applications are industry-specific applications that are developed to serve the particular needs of a specific industry. Common examples of vertical-market applications are those used by the following industries: food service, retail, healthcare, and many others. CRM, SCM, and ERP (enterprise resource planning) software systems are common vertical-market applications.

Vertical-market applications can usually be altered to meet the needs of a specific business within an industry. These applications are more complex than horizontal-market applications because they typically need to be integrated with other systems. Typically, the vendor that sells the application software provides the alterations or provides a referral to qualified consultants to provide the service. Since these applications are more complicated, the business may require the assistance of the IT/IS department for deployment.

Custom-Developed Applications

The third category of application software is custom-developed applications. **Custom-developed applications** are applications that are developed for a very specific and unique need. The IRS is a common example of an entity that has needs that no other industry has and therefore requires software that is developed specifically for it. However, many businesses across all industries may benefit from custom-developed applications if their business processes cannot be changed to accommodate an off-the-shelf software solution.

Custom-developed applications are often perceived as being the most expensive option when it comes to application software. Often that is the case; however, a custom-developed application may lead to long-term cost savings when compared to an off-the-shelf software application that may have lower up-front costs but requires customization or changes in the business process that create disruption and add to the overall cost.

Feasibility Analysis

Many businesses have unique needs and may require custom-developed software to meet those needs. However, it is important to conduct an extensive feasibility analysis to ensure that it is even possible. A **feasibility analysis**, also referred to as a feasibility study, is an extensive evaluation of a proposed project to determine if it is possible to complete with the company's available resources and within various constraints such as financial and legal. A feasibility analysis should be completed whenever a big investment is at stake to ensure that the project can be completed and is profitable in the long-term.

The figure below lists the seven areas that should be reviewed and evaluated in any feasibility analysis.

Technical feasibility

- Existing computing infrastructure is evaluated to determine if it will support the proposed system
- If insufficient, different configurations are proposed and must fall within economic constraints

Economic feasibility

- Most important component of any feasibility analysis
- Determines the costs and benefits of the proposed system with a cost/benefit analysis

Operational feasibility

- Completed only after a project is deemed economically and technically feasible
- Determines if the necessary qualified and experienced human capital is available for development and implementation of the system

Social feasibility

- Determines whether or not you have the support of the end-users of the proposed system
- Examines the probability of the proposed system being accepted by the group that is directly impacted by the system change

Management feasibility

- Similar to social feasibility but focuses on the acceptance by management of the proposed system
- If management does not support the proposed system then it is generally considered non-feasible

Legal feasibility

- Determines whether or not a proposed system infringes on any known legislation, statutes, or even pending legislation

Time feasibility

- Determines whether or not the proposed system can be implemented fully within a specified time frame

Figure 1   Areas to be reviewed as part of a feasibility analysis

When it comes to available database management systems for small to medium-sized businesses, there are several options to choose from, including Oracle, MySQL, PostgreSQL, and Microsoft Access to name a few. Each of these options has a variety of costs to consider beyond the license fees. When evaluating the cost of a system, you should consider the total cost of ownership. **Total cost of ownership (TCO)** is the total estimate of direct and indirect costs associated with a purchase throughout its entire life cycle. For computing systems, the TCO would include licensing fees, tech support, hardware, training, development, and downtime while the system is being implemented.

Business Background

Daryl has provided you with a copy of the database he currently uses to keep track of the gaming competitions that are hosted at Gaming Master. He has also provided you with the worksheet that is currently being used to track the sales. The database is not designed very well and is missing some features that could help Daryl avoid some common mistakes. Also, the Excel file provided has been corrupted and the data will need to be cleansed before proceeding.

Points of Concern

Normalizing the data in this database is critical to avoid redundancy and ensure that it is easily scalable to accommodate Gaming Master as it continues to offer different types of games and host different competitions. Transferring data from Access to Excel and back is one way to ensure that primary keys and foreign keys are assigned to the correct values in the various tables.

Business Requirements

Daryl would like to be able to track reservations and sales in a single database. The single-database solution must include the following features and functionality in order to meet the needs of his business.

- Sales data must be cleaned and incorporated into the database.
- Name of the game needs to be cleaned with the category separated into its own column.
- Customer names should be separated into first, middle, and last names.
- Transaction date should be combined into one m/d/yyyy format.
- All tables must be normalized with appropriate properties and modified for usability and efficient processing.
- User-friendly forms must be created with navigation buttons to allow data to be easily viewed and entered.
- A process that notifies the user entering a reservation in a form when the number of reservations meets or exceeds 110% of the capacity listed for any given event.
- Reports to help Daryl view data about events and sales.
- A Navigation Form to easily access all necessary objects.
- Database properties set to hide unnecessary elements, an appropriate application title, and navigation form to open automatically.

MANAGER'S EMPHASIS
Lookup Fields
Daryl wants to make sure that lookup fields are available wherever possible to avoid typos in data entry.

Provided Files

Game Master's Sales Data 📄 i02SalesData.xlsx	A workbook used by Daryl to track sales at Gaming Master.
📄 i02GamingMaster.accdb	A partial database used to track gaming competition events at Gaming Master.

Analysis Questions

1. The solution you created for Gaming Master is a custom solution that meets the needs of the specific business. However, it is not considered a custom-developed application. Why not? What category of application software does it fall into?
2. What are some reasons that adopting a new DBMS solution such as Oracle would not be considered a feasible option for Gaming Master?
3. Describe your solution to notify Daryl if reservations for any particular event reach 110% of capacity.
4. Explain the process you went through to normalize the data for the Gaming Master database.

Deliverables

1. Submit the i02GamingMaster_LastFirst.accdb database as directed by your instructor.
2. Submit the i02SalesData_LastFirst.xlsx workbook as directed by your instructor.
3. As directed by your instructor, submit the following.

   📄 i02Analysis_LastFirst.docx with your answers to the analysis questions.

   📄 i02Memo_LastFirst.docx to explain and document your solution.

   📄 i02Presentation_LastFirst.pptx to present your recommendations, concerns, and findings to the analysis questions.

   ▶ Post a video presentation to YouTube or other instructor-provided location with a duration of less than five minutes.

Checklist

☐ Sales data provided in the Excel workbook is appropriately cleaned and separated for importing into Access tables.

☐ Tables in Access are created to normalize the data with a primary key assigned in each table.

☐ Field sizes, default values, input masks, etc., are adjusted appropriately.

☐ Lookup fields are created for appropriate fields to reduce typographical errors.

☐ Forms are created to allow for easy viewing of the data and data entry.

☐ A process is developed to notify the user when an event reaches at least 110% of capacity.

☐ Reports are created to display useful data on events and sales.

☐ A Navigation Form is created to allow easy access to the forms and reports.

☐ The Navigation Form opens automatically when the database is opened and other unnecessary elements are hidden.

☐ All analysis questions are answered thoroughly.

☐ The memo thoroughly explains and documents the solution.

☐ The PowerPoint presentation thoroughly presents recommendations, concerns, and findings to the analysis questions, including appropriate formatting.

☐ The YouTube video includes all required steps including appropriate formatting.

☐ All deliverables are completed and named correctly.

Key Terms

Creating Business Analytics for Pricing

REQUIRED SKILLS

1. Create data tables
2. Create named ranges
3. Use queries or Excel functions to cleanse data
4. Use statistical analysis such as correlation and regression
5. Visualize data with charts
6. Conduct what-if analysis

Business Dilemma

Predicting Sales Behavior at Innovative Electronics Using Web Metrics

Production & Operations

The owners of Innovative Electronics are looking to use business analytics to create a competitive advantage and maximize profit. The owners are thinking about changing the default sort order of the company's search results page based on the predictability of the customer to make a purchase. The owners need help to determine if this is possible and to develop an algorithm that would accomplish this task.

MANAGER'S ADVICE ON THIS CASE

"A sea of data can be overwhelming at first. Do not get frustrated or scared to just dig into the data. You may need to run many different analyses to find the proper relationship. You may even want to consider visualizing the data to uncover trends. Also, make sure to keep sample size in mind when looking at data points!"

— Jessica Sobota, Lead Consultant

Files provided by the business:

 i03WebMetrics.accdb   i03LiveData.xlsx (Instructor Provided)

i03Probabilities.xlsx

Deliverable files:

 i03AnalyticsModel_LastFirst.xlsx   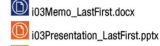 i03Memo_LastFirst.docx

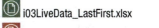 i03LiveData_LastFirst.xlsx   i03Presentation_LastFirst.pptx

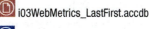 i03WebMetrics_LastFirst.accdb    i03Video_LastFirst

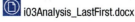 i03Analysis_LastFirst.docx

Understanding Business Analytics

Have you ever had your credit card number stolen? Credit card companies have made large investments in preventing credit card fraud. Through insight, security companies have identified and created mathematical equations to evaluate every purchase's potential for fraud. Using factors such as purchase location, type, and amount, these algorithms compare each transaction to the credit card holder's individual purchase habits. If the equation indicates a high likelihood of fraud, the credit card number is frozen and the card holder is contacted to investigate. This is one example of business analytics at work.

The Definition of Business Analytics

Business analytics is an emerging and developing field from the growing sea of big data available to businesses and is an effort to leverage that data. A search on the web for the definition of business analytics as compared to business intelligence and data analytics will leave most business people as well as students confused. The term is defined differently from one source to another. Some scholars and consulting companies draw specific differences between business analytics and business intelligence. Based on this distinction, the credit card example would be categorized as business intelligence. Others use business analytics as an umbrella term to describe a multitude of analytical skills and tool sets to affect a business's processes or functions, including areas such as data intelligence, data warehousing, and data analysis. By this definition, the credit card example may be characterized as business analytics. Thus, when working with a client or company, communication of how the terms are being used is very important. What you call business analytics may not be what they would call business analytics. This case will use the broader umbrella definition of business analytics.

Business analytics is the process of providing iterative insight to a business by leveraging data through various analytical skills and tools. Business analytics finds relationships in past business data, creates algorithms to predict and optimize, and supports future business functions or processes. In practice, business analytics is a continual, iterative, and real-time analysis that is continually updating and changing based on trends and additional insights gained. Business analytics can influence and change a customer's experience and interaction with a business. Because of the impact on consumers, the speed of the analytics is of utmost importance. Business analytics can be applied to many different businesses' functional areas, such as supply chain, strategy, retail sales, marketing, financial, pricing, and more. Generally, business analytics can be sorted into four different types, as described in Table 1.

Analytic Type	Purpose
Descriptive Analytics	Gaining insight through looking at past data
Predictive Analytics	Using insight to predict future behavior with modeling
Prescriptive Analytics	Using insight to make recommendations with tools such as simulation and optimization
Decisive Analytics	Using data visualizations to provide insight to humans to support decision making with tools such as dashboards

Table 1   Business analytic types

The field of business analytics is growing, and practical applications can be seen everywhere. When you shop at websites such as Amazon.com, the first page contains lists for "you" ranging from "Recommendations for You" to "Inspired by Your Shopping Trends." On video streaming services such as Netflix, videos are presented as recommendations for you first rather than a listing of categories. Some companies are even using analytics to deliver a customized price to each consumer. According to the Wall Street Journal, in 2012, Orbitz found that Mac users spend more on hotels than PC users. Orbitz used this information to start showing different—higher priced—offers to Mac users. Orbitz stated there are not different prices for the same room. Rather, Orbitz was suggesting higher-priced hotel offers and combinations first to Mac users.

This case will provide a framework to apply concepts of business analytics to business practices using the tools provided in Microsoft Excel and Access. In practice, the Information Technology ("IT") used to create and implement business analytics can change quite radically over time. Some of these other tools include separate software such as SAS, SAP, and Tableau. Others are used inside of Microsoft products such as Microsoft BI (Business Intelligence) tools, @RISK, and Solver. Thus, the framework and process of development are more important than the tools being used to find relationships and trends in your data. The skill of how to approach the problem is more important than the skill of how to create a correlation matrix, as described in Table 2.

Common Business Analytics Tools	Examples
Spreadsheets	An Excel spreadsheet analyzing inventory levels
Key Performance Indicators (KPI)	Percentage of business from return customers
Dashboards and Data Visualizations	Sales PowerView dashboard in Excel
Querying	Queries to aggregate sales and pull specific customer types
Statistics	Correlation, regression, and probabilities
Data, Text, and Social Media Mining	Analyzing tweets on Twitter to predict or measure the goodwill toward the business
Simulations and Scenarios	Model what would happen under uncertain variables to determine the likelihood of various potential outcomes
Optimization	Determine a product mixture to optimize profit under supply constraints
Web Metrics	Analyze web data such as operating systems to create a web fingerprint to track customers' habits without requiring a customer login
Audio and Video Mining	Using facial recognition software to identify individuals and product logos in Facebook audio and video to track customers' habits

Table 2   Common business analytics tools

A Framework for Applying Business Analytics

This case involves the use of pricing analytics to determine an algorithm indicating whether a customer is likely to be a high spender or low spender. In order to determine the algorithm, there are several steps you will need to take, similar to those of the scientific process. Beyond the actual process, several studies show that to be competitive with business analytics, a company must embrace a culture of high reliance on analytics that is pervasive across the company and have access to easily shared, quality data. This process comprises the following steps.

1. **Define & Frame** the question to be answered or problem to be addressed.

2. **Collect & Clean** any data that may provide insights.

3. **Explore** the data both mathematically and visually to find insights. Explore trends/relationships between various variables.

4. **Construct your hypothesis** algorithm accounting for all of the significant variables.

5. **Test & Analyze your hypothesis** algorithm using simulation modeling and simulation results.

6. **Test & Analyze live data** for the effect on actual consumer experience and the efficiency of the algorithm. Also, explore new potential insights.

7. **Rinse & Repeat** to incorporate new insights or in some instances even redefine the problem or question being addressed.

Step 1: Define & Frame the Question or Problem

Defining and framing the question or problem is more difficult than one may think. Sometimes the third step of exploring the data only raises more questions and problems that need to be addressed. What should the insight help the business accomplish? How will the insight change the interaction the customer has with the business? How will the insight change or assist a business process? How will the insight support a human decision? The answers to these questions help define the scope and tone of the question or problem being addressed. Table 3 gives some example questions and problems from common business analytics functional areas.

Business Area	Example Question/Problem Definition
Supply Chain	How can the business anticipate when to order more supplies for an uncertain future demand?
Marketing	How can the business provide customized offers and advertisements to customers who will actually be interested?
Retail Sales	How can the business change the user's experience to recommend products relevant to that individual's preferences?
Pricing	How can the business suggest higher-priced offerings to customers who tend to spend more money?

Table 3   Question/problem definitions in various business functional areas

Step 2: Collect & Clean

Data comes in many forms and is regularly incorrect or in the wrong format. The data is not constrained to a single database. Rather, the data can come from a database, a spreadsheet, a web API (such as Twitter or Salesforce data), or any other relevant source. Data cleansing can be a long process. The more cleansing that can be automated with tools such as Get & Transform, new to Office 2016, the better. Although you will need to clean the data for this case, the cleansing portion is not the focus of this case.

Step 3: Explore the Data to Find Insights

Exploring the data to find trends and relationships can be a time-consuming step. The data needs to be evaluated with multiple types of statistical analysis. Further, when a variable is analyzed separately, the analysis may produce different results than when analyzed with other variables. Other variables may turn out to be irrelevant. Further, whether the relationship "makes sense" or is just a coincidence must be considered.

Types of Data

Understanding the type of data is important to discovering insights into the data. First, data may be discrete or continuous. **Discrete data** is data measured across fixed values, for example, quantity ordered or age. **Continuous data** is measured on a continuous scale that can be divided into fractions, such as duration, temperature, or weight. Data can also be subcategorized into the four types of data shown in Table 4.

Data Type	Description	Examples
Nominal	Numbers that simply give the data a label. The order or scale has no significance. Generally, no predictive distribution can be assumed and tools such as histograms are more useful.	What color are your eyes? 1. Brown 2. Blue 3. Green 4. Hazel
Ordinal	Numbers assigned on a scale in which the order is of significance. Generally, no predictive distribution can be assumed and tools such as histograms are more useful.	I would rate my instructor as outstanding. 1. Strongly agree 2. Agree 3. Neither agree nor disagree 4. Disagree 5. Strongly disagree
Interval	Numbers on a scale in which the order matters and the difference between the numbers is measurable. However, interval data does not have a "true zero"—negative values are possible. Thus, ratios cannot be calculated. It can be used in statistical tools that assume a predictable distribution (often, a normal distribution).	Dates Sea level
Ratio	Numbers on a measurable scale with a true zero that allow for ratios—multiplication and division—to be used. The full range of statistical analysis is available. Also, it can be used in statistical tools that assume a predictable distribution (often, a normal distribution).	Income Weight Annual sales

Table 4 Types of continuous and discrete data

Types of Relationships

There are many different types of relationships that variables may share with the outcome. However, that does not mean that the variable actually caused the outcome. For example, suppose data supports a relationship between the height of an elementary student and that student's ability to do well in math. Does a person's height determine his or her math ability? Of course, the answer is no. This is known as the third variable problem. In this case, the fact that the student is getting older and learning in school is the real causal relationship. The student's height is a correlational relationship, as height is related to growing older and not related to math ability. Causal relationships are valuable and provide more information than correlational relationships. However, in business analytics, correlational relationships are still important and useful, particularly when the true causal relationship or the third variable is unknown. In business analytics, the pattern of the relationship is as important as the nature of the relationship. In addition to causality, a relationship may also be described as no relationship, a positive relationship, or a negative relationship, as shown in Table 5.

Relationship Type	Description
No relationship	Knowing the value of the variable does not provide insight on the outcome.
Positive relationship	High values in the variable indicate high values in the outcome.
Negative relationship	High values in the variable indicate low values in the outcome.

Table 5 Relationship types

In the real world, one variable does not always result in a particular outcome. Typically, many different variables all contribute to the final outcome. For example, take the outcome of purchasing a car. The variables that go into that decision are many and complex, including price, quality, and local availability of the vehicle, as well as the individual's perceived social status, nationality, culture, and credit worthiness.

The easiest relationship to interpret and use is a linear relationship. The tools of correlation and regression are very helpful for expressing these types of relationships. Creating a scatter plot of the variables is a quick way to visually see whether a linear relationship exists. Other relationships are more difficult to determine. Sometimes, visualization of the data is the best way to analyze the relationship between variables.

Relationships can exist that look linear but truly are not. For example, take adding salt to boiling water. If one measures the amount of time to boil (the outcome or dependent variable) to the amount of salt added (the variable here, or independent variable), the relationship may look like a negative linear relationship—the more salt added, the faster the water boils—for a while. However, at some point, no matter how much more salt is added, the water will not boil any faster, as shown in Figure 1.

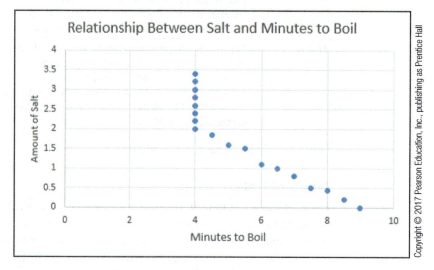

Figure 1   A near linear relationship

Other relationships may be entirely nonlinear and rather curved in some fashion. For example, take the average number of accidents per year by age of the driver. This is a curved relationship in which young and old drivers tend to get into more accidents and middle-aged drivers get into fewer accidents, as shown in Figure 2.

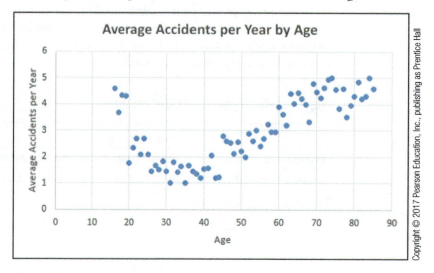

Figure 2   A curved relationship

Step 4: Construct a Hypothesis Algorithm

After all of the existing relationships in a dataset have been explored, a hypothesis algorithm needs to be constructed. This step seems overwhelming to many people. However, "algorithm" is just a fancy word for a mathematical calculation. Often in business analytics, the algorithm should predict some outcome. If the relationship is linear, a regression analysis can easily provide a starting mathematical equation. Other relationships are more difficult to describe. Remember that business analysis is an iterative approach. Thus, the first mathematical expression may not be very good at predicting the outcome. When this happens, explore the data some more and try something different.

So, how "good" does the algorithm need to be? The answer can be dependent on the industry and stakes of the outcome. However, as a general rule of thumb, the algorithm should produce a better result than guessing! So, if the algorithm can accurately predict at a rate of more than 50%, a business should consider it worth using over doing nothing. While a high rate of prediction is desirable, generally an algorithm that predicts correctly in the 60%–80% range is considered very good. Thus, no person should be hesitant to try to develop an algorithm to predict behavior. While many very sophisticated tools exist to help one try to find trends and relationships, very simple mathematical equations that are guided by the intuition of someone experienced in the industry can lead to very successful and profitable algorithms when practically applied, as shown in Table 6. If the relationship appears to be linear, regression analysis is a great starting point.

Example Algorithms	Explanation
PurchaseTotal = (age * 1.59) + (if(Gender="Female",1,0) * 56.26) – 46.7 Type of Purchaser = IF(PurchaseTotal>50,HighPurchaser,LowPurchaser)	Makes a prediction of purchase total and categorizes that customer accordingly
Recommended Books Listed = MAX(#ofPriorPurchasesByGenreOfThisCustomer)	Recommends books from the same genre the customer has purchased the most books from
Exam Grade Score = IF(AND(AverageProjectScores>80%, Class Participation>80%, TimeSpentStudying>3Hours),"Likely to Pass", IF(AND (AverageProjectScores<50%, ClassParticipation<50%, Time SpentStudying<3Hours),"Unlikely to Pass","May or May not Pass"))	Predicts how likely a student is to pass an exam based on project scores, class participation, and time spent studying

Table 6 Examples of algorithms

Step 5: Test and Analyze Your Hypothesis Using Simulation

Simulation analysis is the process of modeling a situation under uncertainty to iteratively predict the statistical probability of potential outcomes. While simulation is a predictive model, it does not predict the future like a fortune teller. A fortune teller would tell a client she will have "three children." Simulation would tell the same client that there is a 10% chance she will have one child, a 60% chance she will have two children, and a 20% chance she will have three children, and it would continue on for all the possible number of children, including no children. In simulation, the model is specific to the situation and not just based on societal averages. The probability that a 45-year-old, childless woman will have ten children is most likely nearing 0%. Simulation is very specific to an individual circumstance. Simulation analysis provides a model to account for uncertainty in a customized and individualistic way. If a model has many assumptions, simulation analysis is more appropriate than analyses such as optimization. Optimizations—such as those using Solver—work best when assumptions are minimal or inconsequential. While beyond the scope of this case, a model can be simulated and then optimized afterward in some situations. Thus, before an algorithm is applied in a practical setting, simulation can help determine the chances that the algorithm will be successful.

Predictive modeling can be done with sophisticated software tools such as @RISK or Crystal Ball. These tools allow the modeler to specify the distribution for which software picks out the variable. This is particularly helpful when the data type is interval or ratio (refer to Table 4). For example, the modeler could say that demand is expected at a normal distribution with a mean of 10,000 and a standard deviation of 1,000. A modeler can determine the distribution based on past performance or based on experience. Excel is unable to do this by itself. However, simulation is still possible using Excel.

The =RAND() function in Excel will generate a random decimal between 0 and 1. The value will change every time the spreadsheet refreshes. Pressing the F9 key will force a refresh to get Excel to generate new numbers. However, most of the time, a variable is not evenly distributed, which is what the RAND function will produce. In other words, there is a 50% chance of getting a decimal of 0.5 and under and a 50% chance of getting a decimal over 0.5. Excel can still use a distribution by using the RAND function with a cumulative probabilities table.

First, the modeler must determine the individual probabilities. For example, suppose the model simulates weekly profit at four potential weekly demands. There is a 10% chance that the demand will be 1,000; a 35% chance that the demand will be 1,500; a 40% chance that the demand will be 2,000; and a 15% chance that the demand will be 2,500. Notice that the percentages all add up to 100%. To create the cumulative probabilities, start with 0 and then add the decimal percentage for the outcome to create a table similar to Figure 3.

	A	B	C
1	Individual Probabilities	Cumulative Probability	Demand Outcome
2	0.1	0	1000
3	0.35	0.1	1500
4	0.4	0.45	2000
5	0.15	0.85	2500

Figure 3   A probabilities table

Then, the modeler can use a RAND() function as the lookup value in a VLOOKUP function across the array of Cumulative Probability and Demand Outcome columns to find the weighted outcome. This method can be used to create hundreds or thousands of individual replications of the model. By generating large numbers of replications of the model, the modeler can recreate the statistical probabilities of the variables for use in predictive analysis.

If the variables are assumed to be independent, then a different random number should be picked per variable. If the variables are assumed to be dependent—for example, in regression analysis—then a single random number should be used to predict the values in all cumulative probabilities variables. For the simulation, the modeler can either use a data table or simply copy down each replication of the model. Generally, a complicated model needs a data table. Here the simulation is used only for picking a theoretical set of variables, applying the algorithm, and then determining whether the algorithm predicted correctly. Thus, the model can simply copy the formulas down without using a data table. Lastly, the model calculates statistics based on whether the algorithm was correct, such as the percentage of time that the algorithm predicted correctly.

Step 6: Test & Analyze Live Data

Once a candidate algorithm is found, the algorithm should be tested using new, live data. If the new data still shows the algorithm as effective, the company can choose to base decisions on the algorithm. Testing the candidate with the simulation should never be enough by itself to implement into the business.

It is extremely important to continually monitor the effectiveness of the predictions. Changing climates can cause an algorithm to suddenly stop being effective. Neglecting to continually evaluate the algorithms in use can actually lead to the opposite of the desired effect! Even missing one day or using poor predictions can cause thousands or millions of dollars in direct losses (sales) or indirect losses (cost of lost profits).

Step 7: Rinse and Repeat and Incorporate New Insights

Even if you monitor the algorithms continually, the company will lose out on potential opportunities and new insights if you stop there. Additional insights can give a company a rare moment to capitalize on for a competitive advantage—agility and finesse are the name of the game in analytics! Like all good business practices, the job is never really done.

Creating Business Analytics for Pricing

The framework for developing the business analytics algorithm provides a starting point. Innovative Electronics wants to tailor search results by whether a customer is likely to make a purchase. If the customer is likely to make a purchase, the results will show the slightly higher-priced comparable items first. If the customer is not likely to make a purchase, as indicated by the algorithm, the consumer will see the cheaper-priced items listed first. This practice has been employed by large online retailers. The ethics of such pricing is not the focus of this case but is nonetheless an interesting question.

Business Background

Innovative Electronics (IE) specializes in mid-to-high-end electronics and accessories—from smart watches to smart TVs. All of IE's sales are made through its website. The owners have read about how analytics can help them leverage competitive pricing. While other companies will actually offer different customers different prices, IE only wants to change the default sort order of products that are presented to its customers on the company search page.

Points of Concern

The data provided for this example is in an Access database. However, much of the analysis will need to be done in Excel. Think carefully about checking the data for errors and putting the data in the proper format and organization for your analysis.

MANAGER'S EMPHASIS

Random Numbers

Very importantly, use only one random number per replication for all the variables when predicting a dependent because a relationship is being assumed.

Business Requirements

The owners of IE need a well-designed spreadsheet model to help them determine whether an algorithm can be developed. IE has provided an Access database containing a subset of 2,000 transactions for analysis. Also, the IT director looked at a larger set of transactions over the past year. From that, he has provided you with cumulative probabilities for some of the data points. If a cumulative probabilities table is not provided, the smaller dataset can be used with a histogram to determine cumulative probabilities. For the deliverables, do the following:

- Cleanse the referral data in the Customers table to ensure consistent results.
- Include relevant correlations, regressions, and/or visual analysis to help determine variables and potential algorithms. You should evaluate at least two different candidate algorithms. If you are unsure where to start, look at your regression analysis.

- Include hypothesis testing using random variables.
- Clearly state the best algorithm and the percentage of time the algorithm was correct in simulation testing.
- Include all considered algorithms, even if found ineffective.
- If directed by your instructor, use the file provided by your instructor to test the best algorithm on a new sample set of live data that has been gathered.
- Include internal documentation of your analysis. For example, use cell comments or text boxes on your worksheets to indicate your thought process in developing your conclusions.
- Use no less than 1,000 replications of the random variable in your simulation model while testing your algorithm.
- For any analysis that you run and find not relevant, copy and place your work in a separate worksheet. Document your results showing why the analysis is not relevant.

Provided Files

Web Metrics Data i03WebMetrics.accdb	Contains, in relational format, a sample of the web metrics data.
i03Probabilities.xlsx	Contains cumulative probabilities for some of the variables compiled over a larger data set.
i03LiveData.xlsx	(instructor provided only) If/when directed by your instructor, this is a subsequent data set for testing.

Analysis Questions

1. What types of analysis did you use? Why?
2. What kind of data was used in the candidate algorithms?
3. Was there a viable algorithm? What analysis led you to this conclusion?
4. If directed by your instructor, how effective was the algorithm on the new data?
5. What challenges did you have in looking for an algorithm?
6. What kind of data was eliminated as insignificant?

Deliverables

1. Submit the i03AnalyticsModel_LastFirst.xlsx workbook as directed by your instructor.
2. As directed by your instructor, submit the following.

   i03LiveData_LastFirst.xlsx

   i03WebMetrics_LastFirst.accdb

   i03Analysis_LastFirst.docx with your answers to the analysis questions.

   i03Memo_LastFirst.docx to explain and document your solution.

   i03Presentation_LastFirst.pptx to present your recommendations, concerns, and findings to the analysis questions.

   Post a video presentation to YouTube or other instructor-provided location with a duration of less than five minutes.

Checklist

☐ Data was checked and cleansed before analysis.

☐ Regressions, correlations, and visualizations were used to explore the data.

☐ Insignificant variables were excluded.

☐ Multiple candidate algorithms were evaluated.

☐ The RAND function was utilized correctly in testing.

☐ All analysis questions are answered thoroughly.

☐ The memo thoroughly explains and documents the solution.

☐ The PowerPoint presentation thoroughly presents recommendations, concerns, and findings to the analysis questions, including appropriate formatting.

☐ The YouTube video includes all required steps including appropriate formatting.

☐ All deliverables are completed and named correctly.

Key Terms

Business analytics   108
Continuous data   110
Decisive analytics   108
Descriptive analytics   108

Discrete data   110
Interval data   111
Nominal data   111
Ordinal data   111

Predictive analytics   108
Prescriptive analytics   108
Ratio data   111
Simulation analysis   113

Required Skills Mapping

Access Case 1:   Examining Business Model Classifications

Required Skills	Comprehensive Book	Business Unit	Chapter	Chapter Title
Work with tables in Datasheet view		1	2	Tables, Keys, and Relationships
Create queries that include aggregate functions and calculated fields	Your Office: Microsoft Access 2016 Comprehensive		3	Queries and Data Access
Maintain records in forms				
Customize forms		2	4	Using Forms and Reports in Access
Use the Report Wizard				
Customize a report				

Access Case 2:   SDLC Basics & Determining Business Requirements

Required Skills	Comprehensive Book	Business Unit	Chapter	Chapter Title
Control the way data is entered with data validation rules, lookup fields, and input masks			5	Advanced Tables
Apply advanced datatype properties to fields				
Use the Table Analyzer Wizard to ensure tables are normalized	Your Office: Microsoft Access 2016 Comprehensive	3		
Create queries with the "most" values				
Create queries that use wildcard characters, advanced operators, and parameters			6	Pattern Matching and Functions in Queries
Create queries that use the Concatenate, IIf, IsNull, Date, and Round functions				

Access Case 3: Anticipating and Answering Business Questions with Advanced Queries

Required Skills	Comprehensive Book	Business Unit	Chapter	Chapter Title
Create aggregate queries		2	3	Queries and Data Access
Create subqueries with business calculations				
Use the Crosstab Query Wizard	Your Office: Microsoft Access 2016 Comprehensive		7	Aggregated Calculations, Subquerying, and SQL
Create a new table using a make table query		4		
Work with update queries				
Create inner and outer joins			8	Action Queries and Advanced Relationships
Use the Find Unmatched Query Wizard				

Access Case 4: Increasing Productivity with Forms and Reports

Required Skills	Comprehensive Book	Business Unit	Chapter	Chapter Title
Create a form from multiple tables			9	Advanced Form Settings and Form Types
Modify the form property sheet				
Modify the form header	Your Office: Microsoft Access 2016 Comprehensive	5		
Modify the form in Design view				
Create a multipage form using tab controls				
Create a report			10	Advanced Reports and Mailing Labels
Modify the report in Design view				
Create a parameter report				

Access Case 5: Developing a Main User Interface for a Payroll System

Required Skills	Comprehensive Book	Business Unit	Chapter	Chapter Title
Create select and action queries	Your Office: Microsoft Access 2016 Comprehensive	2	3	Queries and Data Access
		4	8	Action Queries and Advanced Relationships
Create forms with command buttons		5	9	Advanced Form Settings and Form Types
Create reports			10	Advanced Reports and Mailing Labels
Incorporate logical functions		6	12	Develop Navigation Forms and the User Interface
Create stand alone, embedded, and AutoExec macros				Create a Refined User Experience with Macros

Access Case 6: Implementing a New Inventory Management System

Required Skills	Comprehensive Book	Business Unit	Chapter	Chapter Title
Create select and action queries	Your Office: Microsoft Access 2016 Comprehensive	2	3	Queries and Data Access
		4	8	Action Queries and Advanced Relationships
Create reports		5	10	Advanced Reports and Mailing Labels
Create forms, subforms, and navigation forms			11	Develop Navigation Forms and the User Interface
Create macros to automate and implement complex business logic		6	12	Create a Refined User Experience with Macros
Create VBA Procedures			13	Use VBA in Access
Prepare a database for multiple users and modify the startup options		7	14	Implement Your Database

Excel Case 1: Creating Spreadsheet Models to Support Decisions

Required Skills	Comprehensive Book	Business Unit	Chapter	Chapter Title
Create information with formulas and functions	Your Office: Microsoft Excel 2016 Comprehensive	1	1	Create, Navigate, Work With, and Print Worksheets
Use cell formatting to highlight important values			2	Formats, Functions, and Formulas
Conduct what-if analysis				
Use financial, lookup, and IF functions		2	3	Cell References, Named Ranges, and Functions
Create named ranges				
Visualize data with charts			4	Effective Charts

Excel Case 2: Evaluating a Plan of Action with a Decision Support System

Required Skills	Comprehensive Book	Business Unit	Chapter	Chapter Title
Build nested IF functions	Your Office: Microsoft Excel 2016 Comprehensive	3	5	Complex Conditional and Retrieval Functions
Integrate conjunction functions into IF functions				
Create a LOOKUP function				
Create conditional statistical and math functions				
Use the SUBTOTAL function and filters in a data table				
Develop and customize a PivotTable and PivotChart			6	Integrating Complex Functions into Business Analysis
Work with data and information in data tables				

Excel Case 3: Excel Simulation with Sensitivity and Risk Analysis

Required Skills	Comprehensive Book	Business Unit	Chapter	Chapter Title
Analyze output using a scatter chart	Your Office: Microsoft Excel 2016 Comprehensive	2	4	Effective Charts
Use VLOOKUP and INDEX functions				
Build nested IF functions		3	5	Complex Conditional and Retrieval Functions
Create conditional statistical functions using the AVERAGEIF function				
Use statistical functions such as AVERAGE, MIN, MAX, STDEV.S, and QUARTILE				
Work with data and information in data tables			6	Integrating Complex Functions into Business Analysis

Excel Case 4: Determining Economic Order Quantity and Optimal Product Mix to Maximize Profits

Required Skills	Comprehensive Book	Business Unit	Chapter	Chapter Title
Create information with formulas and functions		1	2	Format, Functions, and Formulas
Create named ranges		2	3	Cell References, Named Ranges, and Functions
Clean data using text functions	Your Office: Microsoft Excel 2016 Comprehensive		9	Organize, Import, Export, and Cleanse Data Sets
Create data tables		5		
Use Scenario Manager				
Create optimization models using Solver			10	Data Tables, Scenario Manager, and Solver
Create and interpret a Solver Sensitivity Report				

Excel Case 5: Creating and Analyzing a Financial Business Plan

Required Skills	Comprehensive Book	Business Unit	Chapter	Chapter Title
Construct a loan analysis with PMT, RATE, and NPER				
Calculate cumulative interest and principal using CUMIPMT and CUMPRINC		6	11	Loan Amortization, Investment Analysis, and Asset Depreciation
Analyze investments using NPV and IRR	Your Office: Microsoft Excel 2016 Comprehensive			
Calculate the depreciation of assets using SLN and DB				
Conduct a basic statistical analysis using Data Analysis				
Predict outcomes using probability distribution functions			12	Business Statistics and Regression Analysis
Find relationships using COVARIANCE.S and CORREL				

Excel Case 6:   Identify Business Trends and Visualize Data with Dashboards

Required Skills	Comprehensive Book	Business Unit	Chapter	Chapter Title
Create information with formulas and functions		1	2	Format, Functions, and Formulas
Create named ranges		2	3	Cell References, Named Ranges, and Functions
Generate descriptive statistics and use probability distribution functions	Your Office: Microsoft Excel 2016 Comprehensive	6	12	Business Statistics and Regression Analysis
Use regression analysis to predict future values				
Incorporate form controls into spreadsheets		7	13	The Excel Data Model and Business Intelligence
Create charts, PivotTables, and KPIs and/or Power View reports				

Integrated Case 1:   Linking Data for Advanced Analysis

Required Skills	Comprehensive Book	Business Unit	Chapter	Chapter Title
Create a new Access table from Excel data	Your Office: Microsoft Access 2016 Comprehensive	1	2	Tables, Keys, and Relationships
Import Excel data into Access				
Save import steps		5	10	Advanced Reports and Mailing Labels
Create an Access report				
Link Access data to Excel		7	14	Implement Your Database
Create an Excel chart	Your Office: Microsoft Excel 2016 Comprehensive	2	4	Effective Charts
Create Excel PivotTables		5	6	Integrating Complex Functions into Business Analysis
Cleanse Excel data		5	9	Organize, Import, Export, and Cleanse Data Sets

Integrated Case 2:   Determine the Feasibility of a New System

Required Skills	Comprehensive Book	Business Unit	Chapter	Chapter Title
Create additional Access tables	Your Office: Microsoft Access 2016 Comprehensive	1	2	Tables, Keys, and Relationships
		2	3	Queries and Data Access
Create Access queries		4	7	Aggregated Calculations, Sub-querying, and SQL
			8	Action Queries and Advanced Relationships
Create Access forms		5	9	Advanced Form Settings and Form Types
			11	Develop Navigation Forms and the User Interface
Create macros		6	12	Create a Refined User Experience with Macros
Use Excel to normalize data	Your Office: Microsoft Excel 2016 Comprehensive	3	5	Complex Conditional and Retrieval Functions
Cleanse Excel data		5	9	Organize, Import, Export, and Cleanse Data Sets

Integrated Case 3:   Creating Business Analytics for Pricing

Required Skills	Comprehensive Book	Business Unit	Chapter	Chapter Title
Conduct what-if analysis	Your Office: Microsoft Excel 2016 Comprehensive	1	1	Navigate, Manipulate, and Print Worksheets
Create named ranges		2	3	Cell References, Named Ranges, and Functions
Create data tables		3	6	Integrating Complex Functions into Business Analysis
Use queries or Excel functions to cleanse data	Your Office: Microsoft Access 2016 Comprehensive	2	3	Queries and Data Access
		3	6	Pattern Matching and Functions in Queries
		4	8	Action Queries and Advanced Relationships
	Your Office: Microsoft Excel 2016 Comprehensive	3	5	Complex Conditional and Retrieval Functions
		5	9	Organize, Import, Export, and Cleanse Data Sets
Use statistical analysis such as correlation and regression		6	12	Business Statistics and Regression Analysis
Visualize data with charts		2	4	Effective Charts

Glossary

A

Accuracy   The most important design principle for creating spreadsheet models. Inputs must be correct to ensure the model's outputs are correct.

Amortize   Refers to repaying the balance of a loan over a period of time in multiple installments.

Analysis phase   The second phase of the systems development life cycle that includes gathering business requirements, creating business process diagrams, and performing a buy versus build analysis.

Annual usage   Required input for calculating EOQ; it is expressed in units and is the known or forecasted demand for the product for one year.

Append query   A query that selects records from one or more data sources and copies the selected records to an existing table.

Application software   Computer program that performs a specific task other than running the computer itself such as an operating system.

B

Bargaining power of buyers   One of Porter's Five Forces; the ability of customers to pressure a company to lower its prices.

Bargaining power of suppliers   One of Porter's Five Forces; the ability of suppliers to set prices for necessary materials.

Business analytics   The process of providing iterative insight to a business by leveraging data through various analytical skills and tools.

Business model   A model that describes the creation, delivery, and retention of how a business captures value.

Business process   A series of steps taken to accomplish a specific goal.

Business process map   A flowchart that uses various symbols to illustrate each step in a business process.

Business requirement   A business need that the new system must include in order for it to be successful.

Business-to-business   Also known as B2B, this model describes commerce transactions where businesses are doing business directly with other businesses.

Business-to-consumer   Also known as B2C, this model is where businesses offer products or services directly to consumers.

C

Capital budgeting   The planning procedure used to evaluate whether an organization's long-term investments are worth pursuing.

Carrying cost   Required input for calculating EOQ; often referred to as holding cost and is the cost associated with having inventory on hand.

Central tendency   Refers to the way in which data tends to cluster around a value.

Choice phase   The third phase of the decision-making process where one of the various solution alternatives is selected.

Clarity   A core design principle for creating spreadsheet models that ensures effective communication of its content to users through the use of formatting, specific text labels, and units of measure.

Competitive strategy   An organization's long-term plan to distinguish itself from various competitors in order to gain a competitive advantage.

Consumer-to-business   Also known as C2B, this model allows consumers to offer products or services directly to businesses.

Consumer-to-consumer   Also known as C2C, this model describes electronically enabled transactions between consumers through a third party. These sites exist simply to connect the consumers.

Continuous data   Data measured on a continuous scale that can be divided into fractions, such as duration, temperature, or weight.

Correlation coefficient   A value between –1 and 1 that describes the strength and direction of a relationship between two variables.

Cost of lost profits   Occurs when an organization suffers a loss of income due to an unforeseen circumstance.

Cost-benefit analysis   Analyzing whether a system development project's benefits outweigh the costs.

Covariance   Calculates the relationship between two variables, like age and dollars spent, as well as the direction of the relationship.

Critical success factor   Allows a business to rank which problems require immediate attention.

CRM software system   A suite of applications, a database, and a set of inherent processes that are used by the business to manage all interactions with its customers from lead generation to customer service.

Crosstab query   A special type of query used when you want to describe one field in terms of two or more other fields in the table.

Crosstab Query Wizard   This wizard helps you to create a basic crosstab query.

CUMIPMT function   Used to calculate the amount of interest paid over a specific number of periods.

CUMPRINC function   Used to calculate the amount of principal paid over a specific number of periods.

Custom-developed application An application that is developed for a very specific and unique need.

Customer relationship management (CRM) A strategy that a company utilizes to initiate and manage the interactions with existing and future customers.

D

Data cleansing The process of finding and fixing obvious errors. Data cleansing is not data verification.

Data flow diagram Maps the flow of data within the organization and its functional areas along with the data stores contained in the system.

Data verification The process of certifying that all data is accurate.

DB function Calculates the depreciation of an asset for a specified period using the fixed declining-balance method.

Decision gate A point in the process where a decision must be made. The next step in the process will be different based on the result of the decision.

Decision support system Also known as DSS, this is a system that helps support the decision-making process and assists the management and strategic management levels of an organization.

Decision theory A theoretical structure for decision making that takes ambiguity into account.

Decision variables Controllable inputs that a decision maker can change, usually within defined constraints, for the current situation.

Decisive analytics Using data visualizations to provide insight to humans to support decision making with tools such as dashboards.

Delete query A query that is used to remove entire records from a table at one time.

Depreciation schedule Records the date that the asset was placed into service, a calculation for each year's depreciation, and the accumulated depreciation.

Descriptive analytics Gaining insight through looking at past data.

Descriptive models Spreadsheet models that are used to describe the current state of a real-life situation.

Design phase (in the decision making process) The second phase of the decision-making process where possible solutions to the problem are considered along with choosing the model to process the data.

Design phase (in the Systems Development Life Cycle) The third phase of the systems development life cycle that includes developing and testing a new system.

Design view A view of an Access object that shows the detailed structure of a table, query, form, or report.

Direct implementation An implementation strategy that involves switching from the old system to the new system at the same time.

Discrete data Data measured across fixed values, for example, quantity ordered or age.

DLookup function A function that is used to retrieve the value of a particular field from a table that meets specified criteria.

Documentation Further explains the purpose of a spreadsheet model and provides any additional information about the model to other people.

Documentation, External Typically in the form of a Word document, includes general information about the model, such as the author, purpose, software used, etc.

Documentation, Internal Descriptive row and column headings, a list of named ranges used, inputs and outputs organized logically, in-cell comments, etc.

E

Economic order quantity (EOQ) The optimal order quantity that minimizes total inventory holding costs and ordering costs.

Economies of scale An economics term that refers to the idea that large organizations can reduce the per-unit costs of an item by being able to purchase large quantities of that item.

Efficiency A core design principle for creating spreadsheet models having to do with the appropriate use of functions to minimize the time and processing power needed to perform calculations and to update the model.

Export Wizard A tool in Access to export an Access database object (table, query, or form) into an Excel worksheet.

Expression aggregate function A calculation that can be performed on summarized data.

F

Feasibility analysis Also referred to as a feasibility study, an extensive evaluation of a proposed project to determine if it is possible to complete with the company's available resources and within various constraints such as financial and legal.

Feasibility study Used in the planning phase, this determines if the proposed solution is feasible from a financial, technical, and organizational standpoint.

Field properties Include features such as field formatting, background colors, special effects, input masks, validation rules, default values, macro procedures, captions and field names, and many more.

Find Unmatched Query Wizard Finds records in one table that do not have related records in another table.

Flexibility A core design principle for creating spreadsheet models that allows a model to be extended or changed easily and utilizes cell references instead of values in formulas and functions.

Form view Data view of a form.

FV The future value of a loan; the balance you want to reach after the last payment is made.

G

Group by aggregate function A function that can help combine records with identical values in a specified field list into a single record.

H

Heuristic A mental shortcut that allows a person to solve problems and make judgments quickly and efficiently.

Horizontal-market application A general purpose application that can be used across a variety of industries.

I

Implementation phase The fourth phase of the systems development life cycle that includes training and conversion.

Importing Means two different things depending on whether you are talking about Access or Excel. In Excel, importing makes a permanent connection to data in Access that can be refreshed. In Access, importing brings data into Access without a permanent connection.

Inputs Known facts about a person, place, thing, or event that affect a situation.

Intelligence phase   The first phase of the decision-making process where information collected will help identify the problems that have been occurring.

Interval data   Numbers on a scale in which the order matters and the difference between the numbers is measurable.

IRR function   Indicates the profitability of an investment and is commonly used when choosing between two investments.

L

Layout view   A view that shows data and allows limited changes to a form or report design.

Lead time   The delay between the initiation of an order and receipt of the order.

Lead time demand (LTD)   The forecasted demand during the lead time.

M

Make table query   A query that acquires data from one or more tables, and then automatically loads the resulting data set into a new table once you run the query.

Mean   The average of all the variables in a sample.

Median   The value that falls in the middle when all the values of a sample are sorted in ascending order.

Mode   The value that appears most often in a sample.

Moving average   Calculates the average of values over time, based on specified intervals.

N

Net book value   Equal to the original cost of the asset minus depreciation and amortization.

Nominal data   Numbers that simply give the data a label. The order or scale has no significance.

Normal distribution   When charted, it takes the shape of a bell curve, where 98% of all values occur within three standard deviations from the mean.

NORM.DIST function   Calculates the probability of an event occurring by using the mean and standard deviation of a continuous variable data set, assuming the data follows a normal distribution.

Nper   The total number of payments that will be made in order to pay the loan in full.

NPV function   Used to determine the value of an investment by analyzing a series of future incoming and outgoing cash flows expected to occur over the life of the investment.

O

Operational management   The first-line managers or supervisors who work in every unit in an organization and are responsible for the daily management of the line workers.

Order cost   Required input for calculating EOQ; often referred to as purchase cost or setup cost and is the sum of all fixed costs incurred each time the item is ordered.

Ordinal data   Numbers assigned on a scale in which the order is of significance.

Outputs   Values of interest that are the result of calculations involving inputs, decision variables, and uncertain variables.

P

Parallel implementation   An implementation strategy where both old and new systems are used alongside each other.

Phased implementation   An implementation strategy that involves introducing the new system in phases.

Pilot implementation   An implementation strategy that involves replacing the old system with the new one at the same time but only for a selected subset of the user population.

Planning phase   The first phase of the systems development life cycle that includes identifying and selecting the system for development, conducting feasibility studies, and developing the project plan.

PMT function   A function used to calculate a payment amount based on constant payments and a constant interest rate.

Population   An entire collection of people, animals, plants, or anything for which you may collect data.

Porter's Five Forces   A framework used to identify the five competitive forces that determine the state of competitiveness in an industry: threat of new entrants, bargaining power of suppliers, bargaining power of buyers, threat of substitute products or services, and rivalry among existing competitors.

Predictive analytics   Using insight to predict future behavior with modeling.

Predictive modeling   The method in which a model is created or chosen to attempt to best predict the probability of an outcome.

Prescriptive analytics   Using insight to make recommendations with tools such as simulation and optimization.

Prescriptive models   Spreadsheet models that attempt to suggest what should be done based on assumptions or standards, and attempt to accurately predict future outcomes.

Print preview   A view of a report or other Access object that shows how it will appear if printed.

Probability distribution   Describes all the possible values and the likelihood that a given variable can be within a specific range.

Process list   A list of steps required to complete the process.

Process modeling   Diagrams created to illustrate a business process.

Property sheet   Allows you to change the characteristics of fields and form parts.

PV   The present value of a loan and is usually the loan amount.

R

Random sample   A subset of a population that has been selected using methods where each element of the population has an equal chance of being selected.

Range   In statistical analysis, the difference between the highest and lowest values in a data set.

Rate   An argument in several financial functions that refers to the interest rate per period.

Ratio data   Numbers on a measurable scale with a true zero that allow for ratios—multiplication and division—to be used.

Reorder point (ROP)   The level of inventory when an order should be made to bring the inventory levels up to the economic order quantity.

Risk assessment   Offers structured information that allows decision makers to pinpoint interventions that can lead to improving a situation or avoiding future problems.

Risk mitigation   Consists of developing options that will enhance opportunities and reduce threats of the choice being made.

Rivalry among existing competitors   One of Porter's Five Forces; the level of competition between existing organizations in the industry.

S

Safety stock The minimum level of inventory that is kept on hand to mitigate the negative effects of shortages due to fluctuations in demand.

Sample population A subset of a population.

Scenario analysis Conducted by changing certain variables to meet a given set of conditions or scenarios. It is commonly used to see the outcome of the most-likely scenario, worst-case scenario, and best-case scenario.

Semi-structured decision A decision that contains both unstructured and structured components, where only part of the problem has a clear-cut answer determined by a suitable process.

Sensitivity analysis Conducted by observing the changes to an output of a spreadsheet model, such as profit, by changing one or more of the variables, such as demand.

Sensitivity analysis Related to what-if analysis, is used to evaluate the impact of a variable on the outcome of a model. Conducted by observing the changes to an output of a spreadsheet model, such as profit, by changing one or more of the variables, such as demand.

Service level The percentage of orders that you want to be able to fill on time.

Simulation analysis The process of modeling a situation under uncertainty to iteratively predict the statistical probability of potential outcomes.

Six Sigma A set of techniques and tools developed by Motorola in 1986 to improve processes in a variety of industries.

SLN function Calculates the depreciation of an asset for one period using the fixed declining-balance method, which means the amount of money that is depreciated is the same for each year of the life of the asset.

Standard deviation The most commonly used statistic for determining the average spread of a data set from the mean and is calculated by taking the square root of the variance.

Strategic management Describes executives such as C-level managers, such as the CEO, CFO, CIO, and COO, along with other senior managers within an organization.

Structured decision A decision that has an organized approach to developing and evaluating innovative options and making justifiable choices.

Subquery A select query that is nested inside another select query.

Supply chain management (SCM) software A wide range of software tools used to manage the interactions along the supply chain from procurement of materials to the sale of the finished product.

Support phase The fifth phase of the systems development life cycle that includes help desk support, maintenance, and system modifications.

Systems development life cycle A methodology composed of five phases that systems engineers and developers use to plan for, design, build, test, and implement information systems.

T

Tactical management Also known as middle management, these managers have not reached the C-level status, but they are not entry-level managers either.

Threat of new entrants One of Porter's Five Forces; the ability of new competitors to enter the market.

Threat of substitute products or services One of Porter's Five Forces; the availability of alternative products or services.

Total cost of ownership (TCO) The total estimate of direct and indirect costs associated with a purchase throughout its entire life cycle.

Type A function argument that indicates when the payments are due—either at the beginning (1) or the end (0) of a period.

U

Uncertain variables Uncontrollable inputs that affect the situation but are not controlled directly by a decision maker.

Unstructured decision A decision that does not have an optimal solution.

Update query A query that is used to add, change, or delete data in one or more existing records.

V

Variance Determines how far the data set varies from the mean.

Vertical-market application An industry specific application that is developed to serve the particular needs of a specific industry.

W

Waterfall method A methodology comprised of a sequence of steps in which the output of each step becomes the input for the next step.

Where aggregate function Allows you to limit the results of your query by specifying criteria that field values must meet without using that field to group the data.

Work flow A series of related topics, listed in chronological order, as they occur throughout the business processes.

Index

Bold page numbers indicate definitions.

A

Access
  answering managerial questions with queries, 17–22
  connecting to data from Excel, 95–96
  creating business analytics for pricing, 107–117
  data, exchanging with Excel, 94–97
  data, exporting into Excel, 95
  data, importing from Excel, 94–95
  data, linking for advanced analysis, 93–100
  data, linking to Excel, 95–96
  determining feasibility of new system, 101–106
  developing inventory management system, 37–43
  developing payroll system, 29–35
  developing phone app, 9–16
  vs. Excel, 20
  increasing productivity with forms and reports, 23–27
  using e-commerce to manage employee schedules and training, 1–7
accuracy, as design principle of spreadsheet models, **47**
algorithms
  constructing hypothesis, 113
  examples of (table), 113
amortize, **76**
analysis phase, **11**–12
annual usage, **70**
append query, **20**
application software, **102**
arrows (business process mapping symbol), 31
as-is business process diagram, 12
assets, depreciating, 76–78
average in model, 64
Avg function, 19
AVERAGE function, 78

B

B2B. *See* business-to-business
B2C. *See* business-to-consumer
bargaining power of buyers, **87**
bargaining power of suppliers, **87**
blank cells in data tables, 64
Bob's Pizzeria's payroll system interface, 29–35
bricks-and-clicks business model, 3
build to order business model, 3
business
  analytics for predicting sales behavior, 107–117
  creating and analyzing financial plans, 75–83
  decision making in, 52–54
  life cycle development systems for, 9–16
  process mapping symbol for decision making, 31
  questions, anticipating and answering with advanced queries, 17–22
  requirements, **11**
  trends, identifying, 85–91

business analytics, **108**
  defining questions or problems, 110
  exploring data for insights, 108–111, 115
  framework for applying, 109–110
  for pricing, 107–117
  types (table), 108
  types of relationships, 111–112
business models
  described, **2**
  four most common, 2–3
business process, **11**
business process map, **30**
business process mapping, 30–32
business-to-business (B2B), 1–**2**
  facilitation of, 5
business-to-consumer (B2C), **2**

C

C2B. *See* consumer-to-business
C2C. *See* consumer-to-consumer
calculating
  NPV and IRR, 77
  reorder point with uncertain demand, 70–71
capital budgeting, **77**
carrying cost, **70**
cases
  Bob's Pizzeria's payroll system interface, 29–35
  CCIB's increasing of productivity with forms and reports, 23–27
  Chloe Jants' financial plan for coffee shop, 75–83
  Collegiate Book Rentals' advanced database queries, 17–22
  County Line Insurance Agency's Excel simulation with sensitivity, risk analysis, 59–67
  Gaming Master's developing a software solution, 101–106
  Innovative Electronics' algorithm to predict sales behavior, 107–117
  Orchard Lawn Care's data analysis and dashboard, 85–91
  Painted Paradise Resort & Spa's employee schedules and training management, 1–7
  Painted Paradise Resort & Spa's phone app for house keeper management, 9–16
  Revolution Bikes' optimization models, 69–74
  Sports Fanatics' inventory management system, 37–43
  Terra Cotta Brew Coffee Shop's spreadsheet model, 45–50
  Tropical Travel Agency's decision support system, 51–57
  Turquoise Oasis Spa's product management database, 93–100
CCIB's increasing of productivity with forms and reports, 23–27
central tendency, **78**
Chloe Jants' financial plan for coffee shop, 75–83
choice phase, **52**